PUFFIN BOOKS

WHO EVER HEARD OF A VEGETARIAN FOX?

Sarah and her older sister Caroline both care passionately about animals. Coming to live in the country, they are horrified by the gamekeeper's traps in the hills around them and set about a secret and daring campaign to sabotage them. But then Sarah meets the gamekeeper's son, Ian, at school and finds him a sympathetic friend who cares about animals too, but in a different way. Ian explains that his dad's work is vital to the countryside and to maintaining the balance of nature.

Confused and frightened, Sarah is drawn into a plan with Ian to track down the saboteurs of his father's traps. And so she finds herself playing the dangerous game of a double-agent – a traitor to her sister and a false ally to Ian. Both of them claim to be doing their best for the animals, but who is *really* right?

Rosalind Kerven is a well-respected author particularly known for her books on ecological themes. She has written several highly acclaimed novels for Blackie and Puffin, including *The Sea is Singing* which was dramatized for BBC Radio Scotland. She has also published several collections of myths and legends and is an established children's books reviewer.

Rosalind Kerven lives in an old stone cottage deep in the wild hills of Northumberland with her husband, small daughter and a very lazy collie dog.

Also by Rosalind Kerven

THE SEA IS SINGING

Who Ever Heard of a Vegetarian Fox?

ROSALIND KERVEN

PUFFIN BOOKS

PUFFIN BOOKS

Published by the Penguin Group
Penguin Books Ltd, 27 Wrights Lane, London W8 5TZ, England
Viking Penguin, a division of Penguin Books USA Inc.
375 Hudson Street, New York, New York 10014, USA
Penguin Books Australia Ltd, Ringwood, Victoria, Australia
Penguin Books Canada Ltd, 2801 John Street, Markham, Ontario, Canada L3R 1B4
Penguin Books (NZ) Ltd, 182–190 Wairau Road, Auckland 10, New Zealand

Penguin Books Ltd, Registered Offices: Harmondsworth, Middlesex, England

First published by Blackie and Son Ltd 1988
Published in Puffin Books 1990
3 5 7 9 10 8 6 4 2

Printed in England by Clays Ltd, St Ives plc
Filmset in Baskerville

Chapter One

Midnight: dark but not silent, full of rustlings, scurryings, stirrings.

'There's supposed to be snakes up here,' said Caroline softly. 'Adders.'

Behind her, Sarah was struggling up the rough path. Something long and dry brushed its way up the leg of her jeans. She stumbled, shrieked, stopped dead.

'Sshh! Idiot! Sound carries from the hills!'

'Caz! You said . . . *adders!*'

'It's all right. I don't think they come out at night.'

'*Please.* Caz, wait for me.' Sarah managed to lower her voice to a quavering whisper. 'There's something . . . round my ankle. Tight. I can't . . . I daren't move.'

Her older sister stomped back down to her, torch-beam prodding the darkness with impatience.

'Honestly, Sarah! It's only a bit of dead grass. Don't be so jumpy. Here, you're free. Now come on, it's not far to go.'

'You keep saying that.'

'I mean it this time. Don't waste your energy. We've got work to do.'

'We've got a test at school tomorrow. It's bad enough . . . but I'll never stand a chance after this and no sleep.'

'We might get a few hours—if you hurry up.'

They trudged on, two lonely silhouettes, dwarfed by the night and the looming, ancient hill.

The path rose steeply, following the course of a small, rushing stream. Its opposite bank was sprinkled with trees: even through the darkness they seemed to be watching, silently disapproving. Sarah hid from them behind a curtain of hair.

Soon the path led them across the water by a rotting plank bridge that see-sawed alarmingly under their weight. Then they came to a high dry-stone wall—and a gate.

The gate was padlocked and someone had painted *keep out* on it in neat white letters.

'We'll have to climb over,' said Caroline. She shone the torch carefully over and around it. 'But watch out, there's barbed wire on top of the wall, on both sides. If you catch something on it, that could be incriminating evidence.'

'What about fingerprints?' said Sarah. 'Couldn't they get us through those?'

Caroline hesitated, running her hands over the weather-battered gate. 'I don't think so. Not on this sort of old wood, surely . . . but that's good thinking. We can't be too careful.'

'No.'

'So perhaps next time we should wear gloves.'

'*Next* time?'

Their eyes met for a moment; then Caroline tossed her head.

'Come on, follow me over.'

The gate creaked and shuddered ominously.

'Help! We haven't broken it, have we?'

'It seems OK,' said Caroline. 'Now look, we go

through the trees next, so it'll be darker than ever. You'd best hold my hand, in case you lose sight of the torch.'

The path here was a mud track, churned up and rutted treacherously by heavy rain-fall and tractors. It was fringed by thick woods. In the distance they smelt sweetly of pine; on the near fringes, dead leaves fluttered down—fingers of rowan, small flutters of birch, like dry yellow moths.

The trees blanked out all the dim glow of moon and starlight.

Caroline shone the torch around.

'Look, let's wait here and have a rest for a minute or two. Would you like a drink?'

Sarah nodded: 'I'm gasping.'

Caroline pulled the back-pack off her shoulders and extracted a small flask of water which she handed to her sister. They leaned against the wall, breathing in the sharp night air.

'I'm sorry about the adders,' said Caroline. 'I didn't mean to scare you.'

'I was just being silly,' said Sarah. 'But . . . the scary bit's just starting, isn't it?'

She gave the flask back to Caroline, who took a long swig from it.

'I keep telling you, there isn't really anything to worry about. How can anyone possibly guess it's us? Now, let's get the cutters ready.'

Caroline pulled two pairs of heavy metal wire cutters out of the pack. She handed one to Sarah. They stuffed them deep into the pockets of their jeans, and Caroline humped the bag over her shoulders again.

'You remember how to use them—OK?'

7

'OK.'

They exchanged wry grins through the gloom.

'Shake hands on it then . . . and Sarah—good luck.'

'Yeah, good luck.'

They walked a short way into the woods. Caroline was counting out paces:

'Forty . . . forty-seven. The first one's here I think.' She swung the torch sharply round. 'Yes!' Her voice sunk with a note that might be relief or perhaps, perversely, disappointment. 'Oh. There's nothing in it. It's empty.'

They squatted together, looking.

It was a snare for catching animals, primitive but effective—a pear-shaped noose hanging about a hand's width above the ground from a thick, forked twig. It was placed carefully across a very narrow animal track that ran off at right-angles into the undergrowth.

'How does it work?' asked Sarah.

Caroline sliced an imaginary finger across her throat. 'Like a slip-knot. It yanks tight—uggh!—like so. There's no escape.'

'Horrible!'

'It is! That's why we're here. Sarah—it's murder. Now you've seen it . . . I couldn't really explain before just how foul it is.'

'Do they . . . die quickly?'

'No,' said Caroline. 'Usually it's slow and lingering. Agony. Sometimes they starve to death, sometimes it's from bleeding—the wire can slice its way through . . .'

'*Don't!* Shut up about it!'

'Well, you asked me.'

Sarah swallowed. 'So. What do we do?'

'It couldn't be simpler. We sabotage the whole

caboodle by breaking it up . . .' Caroline brandished the wire cutters and began snipping recklessly at the snare—'. . . into smithereens. There! That'll get the murderers' fury up! See, it's completely useless now.' She stopped and caught her breath. 'Here, you have a go, Sarah. It's easier to practise on this one, than if we were doing an actual rescue.'

It was harder to cut through the strands of metal than Sarah had expected. *Phit, phit, phit.* Her hands felt sore and aching already. She wondered how she'd cope if an animal were writhing about in it at the same time . . . but Caz would know what to do. She always did.

They crept further along the animal track, crouching to avoid overhanging branches, sometimes doing detours where the undergrowth grew too thick for a human to pass. It was warm and still in the tree-bound dark.

Suddenly there were noises: a muffled scraping, panting . . . shrieking.

Caroline stopped. Sarah couldn't see her face, but the tremor in her voice was enough.

'Sarah! The next trap—there's something in there! Wait here . . .' She crept forward a few paces, then stopped again. 'This one's not a snare—it's a sort of cage. And the . . . It's still alive! We're in time to save it!'

Sarah bumped up behind her, feeling the neatly trimmed ends of her sister's dark, silky hair swinging into her face.

They stood stock still.

Muffle, scrape, pant, shriek, scrape.

'Is it . . . a fox?'

'It can't be. The cage is much too small. I think

they use this kind of trap for other things. Wait here while I look.'

Silence. Then:

'It's a stoat, I think, or a weasel. No—I'm sure it's a stoat. Remember—you recognize them by the black tip to the tail.'

'A stoat!' Sarah crunched her way over the twigs and leaves and crouched beside Caroline to see. A low, oblong wooden box had been placed head-on in the centre of the path. It was about fifty centimetres long. The end facing them was open, but covered with a double mesh of rusty chicken-wire. In the torchlight something small and fierce was crashing angrily about inside.

'But how on earth did it get caught?'

'The other end is open,' said Caroline, 'like a tunnel. I think they put bait inside, then there's a sort of see-saw thing in the middle. The animal runs in, gets thrown into the cage bit and finds it can't get out. Poor little thing!'

'Poor little . . . ? But look at its teeth! They're like miniature kitchen knives! I bet it'll go for us. Caz, we can't possibly . . .'

'It's an animal,' said Caroline heavily, 'a poor defenceless creature, lured into a trap by evil, heartless men. When the gamekeeper comes along, do you know what he'll do? He'll take a stone and smash its brains in!' She grabbed her sister's shoulders and shook her gently. 'Sarah, I thought we agreed about this. Look at it!'

Sarah could feel shivers of fear sweating down her body, somersaulting through her stomach.

'But—but—if we try to free it—supposing it bites us?'

'I'll do it,' said Caroline. She was trembling too, but her voice was steady. 'Don't think I'm not scared, Sarah—but I've got to. Only listen: you mustn't take any risks—it's not fair, I mean, I brought you up here, and you're still only a kid.'

'I am *not!* Not! Not!'

'OK, OK, don't argue, not now. Just stand by. I'll probably—I might need your help. Yes, I do: you'll have to hold the light—hold it steady—I need both hands to work with.'

Sarah took the torch.

Caroline stepped slowly towards the trap. The stoat watched her, clawing at the air. Caroline moved her cutters towards the mesh and slowly, cautiously, began to snip away at the strands of wire.

'Caz! Oh my go . . . Caz, *watch out!*'

'Shut up! Stop wobbling the light!'

'But you can't possibly do—it'll get you . . . be careful!'

She had cut away most of the top now, and was working her way down the sides. Sarah could feel each rasping click as she worked.

All at once there was a shriek, animal-wild, drunk with the madness of sudden freedom. In a flash of brown and white, the stoat leaped forward—and was gone, like a gust of wind.

Sarah blinked. She wrenched her eyes from the broken trap.

Caroline was kneeling on the ground, nursing her hand, sobbing and laughing.

'I did it! I did it! It got away! It's free!'

Sarah rushed to her:

'But, Caz, look at your hand!' Blood was flooding

it, staining the sleeve of her jacket. 'What's it done to you?'

'It managed to bite me . . . poor thing, how could it have any idea I was going to rescue it? It's only revenge, Sarah, *justified* revenge against the rotten humans that made it suffer like that!'

'Caz, there's blood dripping everywhere. It looks awful. You might be bleeding to death! How can you be so calm?'

'How can't *you* be more excited? Don't you see, Sarah, we're fully-fledged animal defenders now. Our first mission—and we've succeeded! I never thought we would. I thought the cutters might not work, or we'd lose our nerve . . .'

Suddenly she glanced down at her bloodied hand. She winced and swallowed.

'Oh! I didn't realize it was as bad as that. It . . . it doesn't really hurt—not *that* much, anyway.' But she was swaying on her feet, as if she were going to faint.

'Sit down.' Sarah pushed her quickly to the ground and forced her head down between her knees. Caz seemed all floppy. She took some deep breaths. The blood was still dripping everywhere.

'We ought to bind it up,' said Sarah.

'Mmmm.' Caroline lifted her head and managed a weak smile. 'There should be a spare pair of socks in the back-pack. Can you find them and improvise a bandage?'

Sarah fumbled for them. 'I'll try.'

The makeshift bandage turned out quite well. Sarah admired it, pleased with herself. Blood seeped through it, but soon stopped.

Caroline stood up and shook herself like a dog. Her

hair shone in the soft torchlight and fell neatly back into place.

'I'm OK now. Let's get home.'

She took the torch and began to lead the way back. Sarah followed numbly. They walked carefully and wearily.

'I couldn't have done it without your help,' said Caroline suddenly. She balanced the torch on a tree stump for a moment and squeezed Sarah's arm with her good hand. 'Remember that. I don't mind taking most of the risks—I mean, it's only fair, part of being older. But you're vital, Sarah. We're a real team.'

Sarah glowed: Caz didn't often find praise for her kid-sister; and because of them, a wild creature that might have died was still alive!

The night noises wove in and out of her consciousness: animal noises, secret, mysterious. In myths, she thought, heroines like them would have been given the gift of tongues, to understand the speech of bird, fox, badger . . . She sighed wistfully. Real life was so hard and complicated: it could never even remotely resemble a fairy tale.

They trudged out of the woods—over the gate, across the rickety bridge, down, down the rough path to the bottom of the hill, across the road—and home.

Home was a country cottage surrounded by hedgerows in the middle of nowhere. There were roses climbing up the old stone walls—and two cars standing guard in the driveway.

Coming off the lonely hills into the metallic shadow of the cars was like slipping from one world into another.

Caroline turned the key silently in the back door. They pulled off their boots and crept in barefoot, holding their breath. The kitchen was welcoming warm and smelt wonderfully of baking: six new loaves were cooling on the table.

Their bedrooms lay down a short passage off the kitchen. Their parents slept at the other end of the long, single-storey cottage: if the girls were quick and careful, hopefully, they wouldn't stir . . .

In her room, Sarah switched on the light, drinking in its brilliance with relief. She shut the door and leaned against it. Her head ached and her mind was spinning. She'd never sleep. She clenched her fists in helpless fury: there was no doubt, she'd do uselessly in her test tomorrow.

She undressed quickly, not bothering to wash or brush her hair, and climbed into bed, sobbing into her pillow. Something soft and furry uncoiled itself from a corner and leaped smoothly onto the bed beside her: it was Aslan, their golden tabby cat. Sarah felt for him and snuggled his cool fur against her tear-stained face.

'Oh, Aslan, Aslan, it was *horrible!* You couldn't bear it—I was so scared . . .'

The night's events spun through her mind like a speeded-up video . . . the woods, the traps, the stoat— oh, Caz's hand! Supposing it was a really deep wound? Supposing it got infected—with something terrible— with *rabies* even! It could be . . . She'd go mad, and die!

Sarah pushed Aslan gently away and forced herself out of bed, stumbling next door. Caz wasn't there. She found her in the bathroom, carefully washing the wound, smothering it with antiseptic, swathing it in sticking plasters.

'It's not too bad.' She grinned at Sarah's concern.

14

'The bleeding's stopped. It's not very big really. Just a tooth mark or two. I've had my tetanus jabs, so there's nothing to worry about.'

Sarah nodded, too tired to fret any more. But Caroline caught her as she was going back to bed, and gave her a big, warm bear-hug.

'I was really proud of you tonight, Sarah, honest. Like I said, I couldn't have done it—not even gone up there—without you. It's really good—we've got a real mission in life now! We'll show those evil animal-killers what's what! Now we've made a start, they won't know what's hit them!'

She stood back and looked her sister in the eye. 'Don't lose your nerve now, will you?'

'No,' said Sarah shakily, 'I'll try not to.'

Chapter Two

In the event, perhaps her tiredness didn't matter too much, as everyone in Sarah's class thought the next day's maths test was impossible and unfair anyway. Bleary-eyed, she handed in her paper with the rest, and trooped out into the lunch-time sunshine.

A crowd was gathering around Ian Metcalfe. There was something vaguely odd about that: Ian was mild mannered, quietly spoken—he was OK, but he usually kept pretty much to himself. Sarah wandered over, curious to see what was going on.

'. . . So my dad's had the police out and all,' he was announcing excitedly. 'Reckons it's that anarchist lot—Animal Liberators or something.'

'But what did they *do* exactly?' asked Karen Bright.

'Smashed up his traps, no less!' said Ian. 'And one of them was dripping blood. Yuck!'

'Human or animal?' asked Danny Harker.

Ian shook his head. 'Don't know. Both, I reckon,' he added darkly.

Sarah poked Karen in the back, trying to look indifferent. 'What's he going on about?'

'Well,' said Karen, 'you know Ian's dad is gamekeeper up on Sir Hugh Harryman's estate?'

'No,' said Sarah. Her stomach gave a lurch.

'Well you ought to,' said Karen, not unkindly,

'seeing as this cottage you've just moved into is bang in the middle of it.'

'Yes, I know *that*.'

'Anyway, part of Ian's dad's job is to trap the foxes and things that eat old Harryman's pheasants and grouse. He goes out checking them first thing every morning to see what he's caught—and today he found the whole lot had been sabotaged.'

'Oh!' Sarah tried desperately to fight off a rising panic. She'd had no idea it was Ian Metcalfe's dad who set the traps!

'Not the *whole* lot,' Ian was correcting Karen. He scratched his floppy mop of dark hair and looked frankly at Sarah. 'Only some of them. But that's bad enough.'

Sarah's mouth felt dry. She couldn't think of anything to say.

'Well I don't blame them,' said Howard Blakey loudly. 'It's about time they made all these traps illegal. I don't know how you can put up with your dad carrying on like that all the time, Ian. Does he *enjoy* seeing animals suffer? Torture, that's what it is—pure cruelty.'

'Hear, hear!' shouted a load of others.

'Fat lot you know about it,' retorted Ian.

'Go on then, give us a lecture on it,' said Cathy Smith.

Ian flushed. 'If my dad didn't trap foxes and the like, there'd be hardly any pheasants left on the hills, and . . .'

'There's hardly any there anyway,' said Howard. 'Old Harryman and his hoity-toity friends from London go and shoot all the ones that the poor foxes miss. What's the difference? Better to let the foxes eat them for dinner, isn't it, than to let brave Sir Hugh shoot them for so-called sport.'

'*Blood* sport,' threw in Louise Platt. 'It's horrible.'

'There's nothing horrible about it,' said Ian. It's perfectly normal and natural. My dad says hunting's as old as civilized man. And that's true, isn't it? *Older* even than civilization, I mean. What about that project on the Stone Age we did last term—they were all hunters, weren't they? It's right for men to hunt.'

'And women!' insisted Karen.

'Phaw!' said Howard, it's bad enough having all these bloodthirsty men doing it. Not women too! They should be at home having babies—not killing things!'

Several girls crowded in to thump him. He ducked away, emerging in between Sarah and Karen.

'Oops, landed next to another animal-hater,' he said, throwing a snide glance at Karen and pretending to recoil from her. She sneered back at him. 'But what about you, Sarah?' Howard asked, 'whose side are you on?'

'I . . . I don't know really,' said Sarah quickly. 'I haven't really ever thought about it.'

'She ought to be on *our* side,' said Karen possessively. 'I mean, she does live right up the dale, near Ian.' She touched Sarah's arm. 'If you haven't worked out yet who really looks after the countryside, it's about time Ian or someone put you right. I mean, it's part of your life now.'

'Oh yeah?' said Howard, 'but you were born and bred in the city weren't you, Sarah? You've only been out here for a few months. So what do they think about hunting and shooting down in the bright lights of Leeds?'

'Well, um, it sort of doesn't arise,' said Sarah. 'You

can't hunt in the town, can you? It's just something you read about in the paper.' She hesitated, choosing her words carefully. 'I mean, you don't even realize it really goes on—anyway, *I* didn't—until you come out here and actually see it.'

'Well, some townies have strong opinions, right enough,' said Ian quietly. 'My dad reckons nine out of ten hunt saboteurs and animal liberators and whatever are city folk.'

'Which just goes to prove,' said Karen, 'that they don't understand—they haven't any idea—what they're about. Sarah's just told us.'

'I haven't . . . I mean, I didn't quite mean that . . . not everyone . . . *some* people understand it, I suppose.' She felt as if she were sliding down a cliff-face, frantically searching for a foot-hold.

'Well, you'll have to make up your mind about it sometime,' said Howard. 'We all of us have strong opinions in this class and we won't let you get away with it. You're not really a new girl any more, you know.'

'Leave her be, with your bullying!' said Karen. 'You animal rights bunch are all the same—bulldozing people into sharing your views. I haven't heard Ian trying to force anyone to agree with him.'

'He's too ashamed of what his dad does, that's why,' said Louise.

'Ashamed?' scoffed Ian. 'I'll tell you what my dad does—he protects the countryside, keeps it nice for all you lot to come and play your ball games in, that's what! Fat lot any of you know about it!'

Chapter Three

The Middle School was in Dalethorpe, a small market town surrounded by hills. Sarah and Caroline lived over ten miles away. The school bus took them there and home again, door to door each day; but it was a long, wearisome journey, winding up and down the lanes to drop off other pupils at farms and villages along the way.

The sisters sat next to each other, looking out of the window, reading. At last they were the only ones left on the bus—except for Ian Metcalfe.

He was half a dozen rows behind them. Sarah could feel his eyes burning into the back of her head, but she didn't turn round. Then she heard him slide out of his place and come swinging down the aisle to the double seat beside them.

He grinned sheepishly, pushing his fingers self-consciously through his jumble of hair.

'You know, seems like we're practically neighbours,' he said.

Sarah nodded, smiling back, but on her guard.

'I mean, I've seen you on the bus these last few weeks,' he went on. 'Which house are you living at, exactly?'

'It's called Rose Cottage,' said Sarah.

'I know it well! Old Watty Tarn used to live there.

My dad helped clear it out. Left the place in a terrible state, he did, when he died.'

'Our parents have done it up,' said Sarah. 'It's nice now.'

'Aye, I'll bet it is,' said Ian wryly.

There was an awkward silence.

'Caz,' said Sarah, 'this is Ian. He's in my class. Ian, this is my sister Caroline—Caz, everyone calls her.'

Ian nodded and gave Caroline a searching look.

'And where do you live?' asked Caroline.

'Gamekeeper's Cottage.'

'Oh! I see.' She turned abruptly and fixed her gaze pointedly out of the window.

'It's less than a mile down the road from your place,' said Ian, still staring at Caroline in a puzzled way. 'You'll have to drop by sometime. Could be good to have someone from school nearby—get right fed up, sometimes, stuck out here all on my own.'

'Thanks,' said Sarah politely.

Ian sat back and chewed his nails for a while.

'Could come and see my collection of animals if you like,' he said.

'Stuffed ones?' asked Caroline coldly.

Ian blinked. 'Huh? 'Course they're not stuffed. They're wounded ones, see. I've got a sort of, um, animal hospital in the back yard.'

'*Really?*' Sarah was genuinely impressed. 'How fantastic! But how do you know about looking after them?'

'My dad knows quite a bit.'

'But I thought—I mean, he's a gamekeeper!'

'Yeah, that's part of his job, see, understanding all about wild animals, knowing them really well—so as he can work out the best ways to control them.'

'Have you got *wild* animals in your back yard?'

'Yup. Only while they're sick, mind. Soon as they're better, I let them go free—wouldn't be kind to keep them. But some of them, they get quite tame, come back and see me and all.'

'But your dad,' said Sarah, 'I thought his job was— I mean, like everyone was saying at school today— doesn't he just go around killing them?'

Ian sighed. 'Aye, you've got hold of the wrong end of the stick—like most folk. It's not as simple as that. He's not some kind of bogeyman! He's really interested in wildlife. Any road, he reckons this hospital thing I've got is good practice for me. See, I want to be a vet someday.'

'Hey, that's just what *I* want to be!' said Sarah. She knew that Ian should be classified as an enemy—but this animal thing sounded really interesting; and on the whole, he seemed quite decent, despite his dad. 'It's supposed to be quite tough to get in, though.'

'Yeah,' said Ian, 'but it must help no end if you've got good experience with animals—and this way, I'm getting it! Then, me and my dad look after old Harryman's labradors too—I'm learning to get them trained as gundogs. But how about you? What animals have you got?'

'Well, there's Aslan,' said Sarah. 'He's our cat.' They both loved him passionately; but it sounded rather pathetic, compared with Ian's wonderful menagerie. 'We used to have a tortoise, too, in Leeds, but he got lost. Our parents aren't, er, that keen on animals actually.'

'My old man hates cats,' said Ian. 'Reckons they're as bad as foxes—going for all the pheasant chicks, and all. Better not let him know about yours.' Seeing

22

Sarah's face, he added, 'Don't worry, *I* won't tell him. None of his business, anyway, so long as it keeps out of mischief.'

The bus rumbled on past the thick hedgerows, turning yellow and scarlet with autumn.

Sarah nudged Caroline. 'Did you hear, Caz? Ian's got lots of wild animals in his garden—sick ones— he's looking after them. He says we can go and see them.'

'Aye, any time,' added Ian.

'Thank you very much,' said Caroline, icy-polite.

Ian raised his eyebrows quizzically at Sarah. 'What the hell's up with her then?'

Sarah flushed. 'Oh . . . nothing.'

The bus swung round a corner and pulled up suddenly in front of a rambling stone cottage.

'My stop!' yelled Ian. 'This is my place, folks. Like I said, drop by when you want. Cheers, Sarah and . . .' He glanced at Caroline, hesitated, obviously decided not to include her in the farewell; and jumped off the bus, swinging his plastic sports bag over his shoulder.

'What a *creep!*' exclaimed Caroline as soon as he was gone. 'What a worm!'

'He's OK,' said Sarah defensively.

'He can't possibly be OK,' said Caroline, 'if his dad's a gamekeeper.'

'*He* can't help that,' said Sarah. Just 'cause his dad's a gamekeeper, it doesn't mean that Ian goes round trapping things, does it—any more than our dad being a bank manager makes us spend all our time counting money?'

'Hmmph.'

A short way further along the overgrown lane, the

bus ground to a halt in front of their own house. Mr Bates, the driver, waved them off cheerily.

'He's a nice man,' said Sarah. 'Everyone's nice around here. Not like Leeds, all busy and grumpy. I'm glad we moved, Caz, aren't you?'

Caroline smiled and tossed back her hair. It was straight and dark, very silky, cut model-style, to chin length. She walked a bit like a model too, very confident, as if she had worldly experience far beyond her thirteen years. She'd always been pretty, always had confidence, ever since Sarah had been old enough to notice . . . and quick—clever too, devouring books and information like sweets. Sarah hung on her every word, respected her opinions; and when Caz made a suggestion she always (little lemon that she was!) automatically obeyed.

They opened the gate and walked up the path. Brilliant clumps of flowers were fading after their last flush in the borders. Their mother had worked hard to get the flower beds looking good for their first summer there. Beyond them, the cottage was an eye-pleasing hulk of long-weathered stone. Fresh white paint on the window frames glinted in the afternoon sun. An abandoned house-martins' nest stuck out from under the eaves and the soft hum of insects filled the air.

'Yes, I *am* glad we moved,' said Caroline. They stood still for a moment, listening to the quietness. 'The whole place is so peaceful . . .'

'Mmm,' agreed Sarah, breathing it in.

'. . . apart from all the animal murderers lurking around the corner!'

'Oh, Caz!'

Caroline tossed her hair again; and Sarah sighed.

Neither car was in the drive. Sarah felt a pang of

24

disappointment. Dad was at work of course; but she hated it when Mum wasn't home to greet them.

Caroline pulled a key out of her purse and opened the front door. They went in, kicking off their shoes to protect the new carpet. It had a luxuriously deep pile, lovely to walk on; if only their mother wasn't so fussy about them bringing in mud. After all, mud was part and parcel of the countryside.

Inside, everything else was new and luxurious too. Tiny sprigs of flowers papered the walls, an antique pine dresser dominated the kitchen, a hand-made wicker log basket stood on red polished tiles by the wood-burning stove. Sometimes the girls wandered from room to room admiring it all, quaint and pretty as a fairy-tale cottage. Their mother was so protective about it, that it really seemed as if one speck of mud or a single grubby fingerprint might charm it all away.

'I wonder where Mum is,' grumbled Caroline, pulling a loaf out of the breadbin. She cut herself a doorstep-thick slice, deliberately, carelessly uneven. 'Want some, Sarah?'

'Please. Not as thick as that though . . . Hey look, she's left a note here.'

'What's it say?'

'*Gone into Gridbeck to volunteer for Village Hall Committee cakestall. Back by five. Help yourselves to tea. Love, Mum.* Oh, Caz, she's getting involved in her good works again!'

'It's the sort of thing you almost have to do around here, I suppose,' said Caroline thoughtfully. 'Small area, not many people, everyone knows everyone else. People gossip like anything in the country, Sarah; I expect Mum hopes they'll all say nice things about her if she volunteers for things in the village.'

Sarah munched on her bread and jam, only half listening.

'So just remember that,' said Caroline firmly. 'People talk. You want to watch yourself more—like on the bus just now.'

'Huh?'

'Getting all friendly with the gamekeeper's son.'

'Honestly, Caz! Don't be ridiculous.'

'I'm not being ridiculous. All it needs is one slip of the tongue, Sarah, one thoughtless word and—kaput! we're in trouble. And what about the animals then?'

Sarah's stomach curdled. But . . . it had all seemed so simple, so sensible at first. They'd always been mad keen on animals, had often talked about how good it would be to dedicate their lives to helping them. Then when they moved here and started exploring the hills, they'd stumbled on some traps—and realized that here they were, bang in the middle of a terrible cruelty, one that seemed dead simple to put right. Caz had read up about it, made meticulous plans . . . it had never occurred to Sarah that it might be really risky; or that it might overlap into normal, every-day life, get in the way of things, even stop her making friends.

'Surely,' she said slowly, 'if I was rude to him—that would give him more reason to be suspicious?' She hesitated. 'Anyway . . .'

'Anyway what?'

'He's OK. I mean, he *is* friendly—and, well, you heard what he said, he's really interested in animals—like us.'

'Like us? Don't you realize, Sarah, his dad's the arch-villain! How can he be like us?'

'He wants to be a vet,' said Sarah pleadingly, 'and so do I. He seems to know quite a lot. He's got this

26

animal hospital. He could be interesting to . . . to talk to.' She hated arguing, but this time Caz was really going over the top. She threw her a defiant glance. 'I bet he knows more about animals than you do.'

The colour rose in Caroline's cheeks. She swallowed, and said in a throaty voice:

'Sarah, please don't start going round to that boy's house. It would be like—it is—being friends with the son of a torturer. Just imagine, you could be talking to him in one room—and his father setting traps maybe just through the door. How could you bear it?' She put a hand on Sarah's shoulders. 'For the animals' sake, Sarah, not for me. Please.'

'I don't tell you who to be friends with,' said Sarah tightly.

'I wouldn't care if you did. And . . .'

'No! Because you'd take no notice.'

'. . . and anyway, I choose my friends carefully. That's why I go round with Emma and Jenny, because I know they've got strong moral principles too. In fact . . .'

'Moral principles! They why don't you take them out on your rescue missions instead of dragging me?'

Caroline looked at her seriously.

'Oh, Sarah, we're sisters—that makes us special! It means we can really trust each other. I mean, I really like Emma and Jenny, but I haven't known them that long. Besides, they both live miles away in town and . . .'

'Oh. So you're just making use of me because I happen to be on the spot.'

'What's got into you? I always thought you wanted to help the animals as much as I do.'

Sarah pushed her plate away with a sigh.

27

'Yes. But . . . I don't want it taking things over. I didn't realize, when we talked about it before, just how serious—how dangerous—it is. I need to . . . to think about it, Caz.'

'Look, if something about it's bugging you, Sarah, just tell me. Let's talk about it together. Talking's much better than thinking.'

A lump rose in Sarah's throat. She shook her head.

Chapter Four

It only took Sarah quarter of an hour to walk to the Gamekeeper's Cottage on Saturday. All the way there, she kept saying to herself, I ought to go back, I must be crazy; but a stubborn determination not to be dictated to by Caz kept her going.

The gate was secured by a well-worn latch and chain like the field gates. While she was fiddling with it, what sounded like a whole kennel full of dogs set up a barking.

They must know in the house that she was there! Flushed, she looked up at the windows, but they all stared blankly back at the sun. Perhaps if she turned and ran now . . . but no, she had to see this through. Anyway, there was no reason to snub Ian.

She got the gate open and closed behind her at last, and crunched up the drive, skirting a mud-spattered landrover that was parked in the middle. There weren't many flowers in the Metcalfe's front garden, most of which was taken up by a large, very well tended vegetable patch surrounded by soft fruit bushes. She could see a great clump of ripe black-berries and her mouth watered.

She set her face and pressed the bell.

There was more barking—from indoors this time— and unhurried footsteps. She composed herself, expecting she would have to face Ian's mum.

But it was Mr Metcalfe himself who opened the door.

'Yes?' He sounded vague, but not unfriendly, a big, beefy man in very grubby jeans and a patched-up sweater, trainers on his feet. His hair was a dark, unruly mop, like Ian's.

'Um, is Ian in please?' Sarah's cheeks were burning and her voice came out all silly and squeaky.

'Aye, he's in all right.' His face cracked into a half-smile: Sarah had the feeling he might be teasing her, though perhaps not unkindly.

'He said to call. He said any time would be OK. To see his animals.'

'Ahah!'

'I live just down the road, you see.'

'Aye, I've seen you all right! John Carr the bank-man's lass, aren't you? Nice how you've done the little place up. Eveyone's talking about it, you know.'

'I . . . I'm in Ian's class at school,' said Sarah lamely.

Mr Metcalfe stretched lazily. 'Well, I'll give the lad a shout. Come in—er—?'

'Sarah.'

'Sarah, that's it. Well come along in then.' He turned and yelled into the depths of the cottage: 'Ian! I-an! Lass to see you! Don't keep her waiting now.' There was no response. He winked at Sarah. 'Look, if you walk through that door there, and then straight on through the one behind it, you'll find him. In the yard. Nose stuck in those cages of his, no doubt. Off you go.'

Sarah swallowed, stepped into the cottage and opened the door Mr Metcalfe pointed at. It led into a big kitchen, a bit shabby and old fashioned, but filled with a comforting smell of bacon and jam. A large, suntanned woman wearing an apron over outsize jeans, was busy at the sink.

'Could you just pass us the sharp knife, love,' she called, without turning, as Sarah went in.

Sarah coughed nervously. 'Um, please . . . I'm not . . . I'm sorry, my name's Sarah. Your . . . Mr Metcalfe sent me in here—I'm looking for Ian.'

Ian's mum spun round, laughing in surprise. 'Oops! I'm sorry, my love—I had no idea! One of Ian's school mates, are you? Oh, *I* know, aren't you one of those new Carr girls? Of course! Well, nice to meet you.' She beamed, started to offer a damp hand covered in vegetable peelings, then thought better of it.

'You'll find Ian through there—' (she pointed to the back door) 'stuck with those wounded animals of his, as usual.' She had a nice face, Sarah thought, battered but calm. 'Just walk straight out.'

The back door opened onto a largish paved yard with weeds pushing up through the cracks. It was surrounded on three sides by crumbling dry-stone walls. Along the longest walls were ranged some home-made cages, all grey wood and wire netting, a variety of shapes and sizes. In front of one of the cages, his back to the door, stood Ian.

Sarah coughed again. 'Hello.'

Ian took his time to finish whatever it was he was busy at, snapped the cage door shut and turned round to greet her.

'Hi. You decided to come after all then.' He peered round her. 'Left your grumpy sister at home, have you?'

31

'Yes,' said Sarah firmly. 'What's in the cages?'

'There's a little bat in this one.'

'A *bat?*' Sarah shuddered.

'Broke its wing,' said Ian. 'Mum found it in the coal shed yesterday—must have lost its hold on the rafters there when she slammed the door shut. All bloody it was. I've cleaned it up though. Want to see?'

Sarah went over and peered through the wires. The bat was smaller than her hand. Upside down, it clung to a strut across the top of the cage, trembling slightly, letting out miserable, high-pitched squeaks. Its body was covered in brown fur that looked as if once it might have been soft and beautiful, though now it was all bedraggled.

'Like the splint?' said Ian. 'Matchsticks and bandages. My own design. Not bad, huh?'

'Look at its teeth!'

Ian laughed. 'Aye, just look at 'em! Hey, it's feeding time. Want to help?'

'What do you give it?'

'Insects, mostly.' From underneath the cage he pulled out a large, screw-top jam jar with holes punched in the lid. It was brimful with flies, gnats and midges, some dead, some still squirming around.

'Ugh!' gasped Sarah. 'This'll give me nightmares!'

Ian raised an eyebrow at her. 'But I thought you were keen on animals too?'

He opened the jar and sprinkled a generous helping of flies into the cage. The little animal snapped at them hungrily.

'On the bus,' Ian persisted. 'You said you wanted to be a vet like I do. Can't be squeamish if you really want to be one.'

'No,' said Sarah humbly. 'What else have you got here?'

'Nothing much at the moment. Just a couple of young grouse.'

'Grouse? But why should you want to ... I mean, your dad shoots them, doesn't he?'

'I should hope not!' said Ian. 'Old Sir Hugh would go bananas if he did. Dad's job is to *look after* the things, keep them alive and healthy and breeding and all that, so as Harryman and his mates can shoot them.' He looked carefully at Sarah. 'Sounds daft, does it?'

'Well, since you ask—yes.'

'No different from breeding lambs or chickens for the slaughterhouse though, is it?'

'I ... I don't really know enough about it.'

'Hey, Sarah, please don't be like all them half-wits at school. Think about it. *Now*. Shooting game birds is no different from farming—right?'

'But surely ... I mean, grouse are wild, aren't they?' said Sarah carefully.

'Aye, lucky things! Better wild than stuck on a factory farm, hey? Anyway, these are the ones. Dad found them half starving on the moors. Got some sort of disease—worms, we reckon. Given them some medicine, now I'm trying to feed them up. See, it's a bit of an experiment. When they seem strong enough, we'll release them back into the wild.'

'To be shot,' said Sarah wryly.

'Not necessarily,' said Ian. 'Only quite a small number gets shot actually. The rest stay alive and keep breeding, have more chicks next year. Has to be like that, or soon there'd be no grouse left to shoot, would there?'

'Hmm,' said Sarah.

Ian snapped the cage door shut and turned to face her.

'I'd best be going,' said Sarah awkwardly.

'I could show you a badger sett—if you're interested, that is,' said Ian.

'Badgers? Oh *yes!*' She'd always wanted to see one. 'Where is it?'

'Just over the wall,' said Ian. 'But you mustn't tell anyone about it.'

He led the way to a corner of the yard, heaved himself onto an old dustbin and scrambled over the head-high, crumbling stones, dropping down the other side. Sarah followed.

They landed in a patch of ancient beech wood, all fat trees and leaf-mould underfoot. In the still air, golden-brown leaves were floating softly down.

Ian stopped abruptly.

'Listen: swear you won't tell anyone I showed you this, Sarah. There's not many know. I shouldn't really . . . dunno why I'm trusting you. No. Perhaps I won't.'

'Oh Ian, *please!*' She couldn't bear to miss out on such a chance. 'I *love* animals—more than anything.'

Ian hesitated, scuffing up the rich, damp earth with his toe.

'Yeah. They all say that. But one thoughtless word . . . There's people come out here digging, see. Badger baiters. Set their dogs on them, tear them to pieces.'

'You mean that sort of thing goes on around *here?* But this is the heart of the country—it's miles from anywhere!'

'Yeah, well—new girl. You'd be amazed, maybe,

at the crime my dad knows about. There's money tied up in it, see—they put bets on which animal gets torn to pieces first. It's city thugs, mainly, drive out here specially. Just like the poachers. Sadists, they are, just wanting to get animals *hurt.*' He grabbed her arm with sudden fierceness. 'Swear it, Sarah, swear you won't breathe a word about these badgers.'

'Of course I won't tell anyone, stupid!'

'Not even that rat-bag sister of yours?'

'Caz? But she wouldn't—she loves animals too. They're our . . . well, we just want to help them.'

'OK, OK, but I want you to swear it properly.'

'All right—cross my heart and hope to die—I won't tell Caz, or anyone else.'

Ian relaxed a bit and walked on, leading her to a tree whose roots formed the entrance to a large hole.

'It's down there,' he said proudly, as if he owned it. 'This is the main way in—their front door, like. See all the bits of bracken in that pile of earth—that's their old bedding, stuff they've chucked out. And this here's their scratching post, see?'

He pointed to a nearby tree. Much of the bark was scraped off and there were long, deep claw marks in the wood. Some of them looked quite fresh.

'And here's the dung-heap. They're very clean, badgers—always go outside.'

'Have you ever actually seen them?' asked Sarah.

''Course. Lots of times. I suppose I could show you, if you wanted. But you'd have to be here around midnight. That's the best time.' He shot her a pitying glance. 'Not much chance of that, I reckon. Girls can never stay up.'

'What a cheek!' cried Sarah. 'I was up at midnight

only the other day! I . . .' Too late, she stopped herself.

'Oh aye,' grinned Ian. 'Doing what, eh? Swotting for your test, I'll bet!'

'I was *not!* I was . . . out.'

'Pull the other one,' said Ian.

It was getting to be dangerous, this talk; but to her horror, Sarah found she was enjoying it. It was like a game: in a weird way it was exhilarating, like biking too fast on the wings of a gale. She ought to stop now, she knew . . . but a little demon inside forced her on.

'I was on the hills,' she said recklessly, 'so there.'

They were walking back to his yard now. She waited for him to respond, to challenge her about what she was doing; but all he did was to guffaw disbelievingly.

'Right, we get back by climbing over this tree here,' he said. His look was mocking, challenging. 'Do you *really* want to meet me for some badger watching?'

'Yes! When?'

'Tomorrow then. Midnight, like I said. Here.'

'OK.' Sarah bit her lip.

'And don't breathe a word to your sister.'

She scrambled down after him into the yard.

Mr Metcalfe was waiting for them. 'Aha, the prodigal son returns home! You promised to exercise the dogs this afternoon, Ian. So where have you been?'

'Just showing Sarah the badger place,' said Ian.

'Oh aye.' He turned to Sarah pleasantly. 'Interested in animals, are you, Sarah?'

She nodded. She felt like a baited badger herself.

Watch what you say, don't trust him ... A little voice that sounded disturbingly like Caz's was drumming inside her head. Yet when you actually *saw* him, *spoke* to him, it was difficult to identify the gamekeeper as the bloodthirsty villian that Caz had made him out to be.

'Well, if you're potty about wildlife like my lad is,' said Mr Metcalfe kindly, 'don't hesitate to ask if there's anything you want to know. Count myself a bit of an expert, see. It's my job. Had a lifetime of observation.'

Sarah took a deep breath. OK, she wouldn't let the side down. She'd face up to him: she'd find out as much as she could.

'Please,' she said carefully, 'do you think you could explain ... about gamekeeping and that. I mean, what do you actually do? What's the point of it? I know you look after the pheasants and grouse and things, but why—just so as people can shoot them?'

Mr Metcalfe looked her straight in the eye. Below his thatch of hair he had a ruddy face and thick lips that perpetually seemed to be almost grinning.

'Well, the folks that shoot 'em reckon as it's good fun,' he said blankly.

'Fun?' cried Sarah.

'Satisfies a basic human instinct, that's my theory,' said Mr Metcalfe. He was obviously warming to his subject, the words came tumbling out as if it were his favourite hobby-horse. 'See, man's always had an urge to hunt. Without it we'd never have survived in primitive times. Well, now folk are mainly stuck out in the cities ...' He shook his head distastefully '... some of them, they keep getting this primeval urge, a sort of itch maybe, to be out after the game, like they're still biologically programmed to be.'

Sarah stared at him: it was impossible to tell how much he was really teasing her.

'Anyway, game's nice to eat, you know. Ever tasted pheasant or grouse?'

She shook her head.

'Have to try and get a brace up to you some time. Look at it this way, Sarah: the shooting's just a good bit of sport—and you get something nice and tasty for the pot at the end of the day.'

'Oh.' Sarah's head was buzzing with arguments, but she didn't dare say anything.

Mr Metcalfe folded his arms. Now he was quite obviously being serious.

'Sometimes we get city folk out here for their picnics,' he went on, 'and when they find out about the shooting, they get all hoity-toity and say' (here he put on a posh accent) '"Ooh, you shouldn't shoot *wildlife*, you know." Makes me right mad, that does! If it wasn't for me looking after the hedgerows and the woodlands, burning the moors each year to keep the heather nice and healthy, there wouldn't *be* any wildlife worth mentioning for them to come and trample over. Daft pig-heads they are! Any folks with views like that ought not to eat *any* meat, I say—else they're nowt but damn hypocrites. "Right," I say to them, "then I hope you live up to your beliefs by being a vegetarian?" No answer to that, most of them. Eh, Ian?'

Ian grinned back at his dad.

'But what about . . . I mean, don't you trap foxes and that sort of thing?' said Sarah. 'Don't . . . don't these sort of people criticize you for that?'

'Ah,' said Mr Metcalfe softly, 'old Foxy now. He's

a right wily character, Sarah. Haw! Talk about clever, talk about sly! All them fairy tales you hear about foxes, lass, they're all based on fact. Fascinating character the fox. If I didn't have to earn my family a living, I could easily spend a lifetime studying him.'

'But instead . . .' she tried to sound calm and pleasant about it '. . . you *kill* them.'

'Aye. Ever seen the damage a fox can do in a coop of broody pheasants? Kill every bird and every chick in sight, he will, smash up every egg, just for the fun of it! Then maybe his lordship or her ladyship—the vixens can be even worse—will deign to carry just one bird away to eat and leave the rest of the mess for me to clear up. Talk about bloodthirsty, talk about cruel! You want to hear those birds scream! Ask any farmer with a few chickens, he'll tell you just the same.

'See, nature's just as cruel as man is, Sarah, but there's lots of folk don't see it like that. We're no worse than any other meat-eating animal—no better either, I'll admit that.

'We're in the same daft business, Fox and Man, when it comes down to it—both trying to rule over our own corner for a good meal and a bit of sport. Listen, I *respect* the wild ones, Sarah, I'm not trying to wipe them out or anything! My job's just to cull them, to keep their numbers down that little bit, so as the birds in my charge can flourish. That way, other creatures can flourish a bit more too, by the by: songbirds and rabbits, shrews and voles—all the small ones that foxes and rats and weasels like to eat

'Mind you, sometimes it's not that easy, I can tel

39

you. Sometimes I reckon as *they're* the clever ones, not me.'

'Yes,' said Sarah, 'I think I see.'

His speech had made her all squirmy and uncomfortable inside. There was something about Mr Metcalfe: he belonged to the hills properly. He wasn't just an observer, like her and Caz. He wasn't sentimental about the animals: you couldn't be, she could see that, not in his job; but he seemed in tune with them somehow. He was fighting a sort of quiet war, which neither side could ever win, because the enemy—the foxes and stoats and so on—were maybe in their way as cunning as he was.

It gave her a shivery feeling to think of it—and a deep longing to get really close to nature, like he was.

Maybe she just hadn't been born the right way. Maybe she and Caz cared about animals—about individual animals—too much.

'Well!' Mr Metcalfe gave Ian a hearty slap across the shoulders, 'there's them hounds waiting to be off. Come on, Sarah, we'll show you the way out past the kennels.'

He led the way through a narrow iron gate in a corner of the yard and down a rough drive towards a long, low building. As they approached, the chorus of dogs began to bark again.

'How many have you got?' she asked in wonderment.

'About a dozen,' said Mr Metcalfe matter of factly. 'They're Sir Hugh's gun dogs, see. Part of my job to look after them.

'Look lass, if you're on your way out now, I'd be glad if you'd go quickly through the main gate and shut it tight behind you first. Don't want them getting on the road, or anything. Most of them's obedient and good as gold, but one or two's still barely pups and . . .' he clouted Ian affectionately round the ear '. . . this lad insists he's working on them, but if he doesn't get on with it, they'll be untrained till kingdom come!'

Sarah didn't stop to argue. She ran down to the gate and out, then pulled it to, locking its chain firmly on the hook.

She saw Ian go to the door of the kennel, open it—and then there was a thundercloud of black and golden labradors milling around the drive, all of them barking madly.

Safe on the other side of the gate, she called:

'Hey Ian! Is it definitely on about the badger watching tomorrow?'

He came half way towards her and shrugged.

'It's up to you. But come quietly. And you'll have to leave your lights behind.'

He turned back to the dogs.

'I'll be there!' she shouted at him.

But she wasn't sure if he heard—or indeed, whether he even cared.

Chapter Five

Sarah was lying on her bed, idly admiring the careful arrangement of posters which adorned the walls of her room. There was a chart of *Native Wild Animals*, another showing *Butterflies of the World*, a huge blow-up of a cat that looked exactly like their own Aslan and a large collection of postcards of animals and birds. Even her curtains were patterned with cats in various rather coy, chocolate-box poses. OK, she had to admit they were rather babyish now, but she still liked them . . .

She was disturbed from her daydreaming by a tap on the door. Caroline came in with Aslan at her heels. She closed the door tightly and sat down on Sarah's bed. She was clutching a sheet of paper.

'What's up?'

'This,' said Caroline grandly, unfolding the paper and holding it out to show her, 'is a map.' She cleared her throat. 'A map of all the game-bird territory within two miles of here and where I reckon the traps are—most of them, anyway.'

It was a neatly-drawn sketch-map complete with scale. Sarah blinked at it admiringly.

'Brilliant, Caz! However did you do it?'

'Oh, the drawing was easy.I just copied Dad's big Ordnance Survey map. The traps . . . well, I've been out walking and looking. You soon get to guess where they might be. It's just like it says in that big book I got from the library—remember it? Most of them are along well used animal runs—low, narrow paths through the woods and along the hedgerows. It's pretty grim, Sarah. You'd be amazed how many there are. The whole area round here is like one big torture chamber!'

Caroline waited while Sarah studied it. Then she said:

'So that's the map. Now here's the plan.'

Sarah groaned inwardly. 'What plan?'

'I reckon we could manage to sabotage maybe a dozen snares and cage things in an hour, if we choose ones that are quite close together. One night a week is probably as much as we can cope with. We could get through loads of them at that rate, make sure a large proportion are out of action at any one time.'

'But the gamekeeper will just keep on mending them,' said Sarah.

'Don't be so defeatist! Come on, Sarah, it was really good last time—really exciting when we freed that stoat. I thought we could have the next go tomorrow night, if the weather's OK.'

Oh no! Tomorrow night Sarah was supposed to be badger watching with Ian. He wouldn't think much of her if she didn't turn up. It was even possible, when his dad found more broken traps ... he might get suspicious. Besides, she was really desperate to see the badgers.

'Why does it always have to be at night?' she asked carefully.

'It's safest under cover of darkness.'

'But *is* it?' A new idea struck her: she seized it

gratefully. 'When it's dark, you can't see where you're going properly, or what you're doing, what tracks you're leaving behind—or who's following you.' She warmed to the logic of her argument. 'And then what about the torchlight? Ian's dad—the gamekeeper—I think he works all hours: he's bound to be on the lookout for ... well, for, um, saboteurs—us—and poachers and things. A light on the hills must stand out for miles.'

Caroline sighed. 'Yes, I see your point. Hmm. I suppose it *is* a bit of a risk. But if we do it during the day, it could only be at a weekend.'

'That's much better,' said Sarah. 'At the weekend it could be anyone—people driving out from the city, from miles away. It'll help keep the suspicion off us.'

'Ye-es. But then the thing is, there's more risk of bumping into the gamekeeper during the day.'

'But is it more of a risk really? I mean, loads of people go walking on the hills, surely it's quite normal for us to be out. I mean, we do live here. It's much less suspicious than being caught at night.'

'I suppose so.' Caroline sounded as if she needed more convincing.

'So!' urged Sarah, 'tomorrow night's off—yes?'

'Well, all right. We'll try it once during the day—this next weekend—and see how it goes.'

Caroline sat down on the bed and began leafing idly through some of Sarah's books. The cat jumped up too and wormed his way into her arms with a great sigh of contentment. Caroline stroked him with a smile, almost purring too.

'Caz,' said Sarah, 'I've been thinking. If we're, um, animal liberators and that, don't you think that maybe we shouldn't eat meat?'

44

Caroline looked at her thoughtfully. 'I know exactly what you mean. I've been wondering about that a bit too. Like: what goes on when they slaughter the animals? How can the man with the knife—or whatever they use—how can he bear to *kill* them? Doesn't it hurt? It must do. They must be—the animals I mean—so scared! They must know what's going to happen.'

'Imagine a cow looking at you, pleading and terrified,' said Sarah, 'or a lamb. And then—oof—they've killed it—and we end up eating it. But it's not just that: what about factory farming? Battery hens cooped up in cages too small to turn around in, and calves kept indoors all the time in tiny, dark cells.'

Caroline shuddered.

'I've been thinking about it quite a lot since we've lived here,' Sarah went on. Her mind flitted back to Mr Metcalfe's scathing remarks about city 'do-gooders' who ought to be vegetarian; but it was no business of Caz's where the idea had come from. 'I suppose when you see the animals around you all the time, you start to realize what it's all about. It's horrible. I mean, all the dear little lambs growing up in the fields all through the summer, and then before they even have time to finish growing, we end up eating them for Sunday lunch! Actually, I think it's *worse* than Sir Hugh Harryman eating pheasant or grouse, Caz—at least they're free, they're wild—until they get shot, and they do have a small chance of escaping.'

'The trouble is,' said Caroline, 'that I really like eating meat. I'm sure I'd miss it if I gave it up.'

'But you're the one who keeps on talking about making sacrifices for the sake of the animals!' cried Sarah. The truth was, she herself didn't like meat very much anyway. She honestly couldn't care less if she never ate it again. It made her feel sick to see Mum handling it—raw lumps of red flesh, or beheaded chickens, their poor bodies all pale, plucked and goose-pimply.

It felt good to take the lead, for once, over Caz. And it helped allay the nagging guilt she felt about her secret visit to Ian.

Caroline got up, still cradling Aslan, and looked out of the window. There was a fantastic view: over-the-hills-and-far-away, like in a holiday brochure. Sheep were grazing in the field across the road. She sighed again.

'I guess you're right, Sarah. We've really got to give up meat if we're going to be true to our principles. We'll tell Mum. Whatever do you think she'll say?'

'We ought to think it through properly though,' said Sarah. 'What about eggs—and milk and cheese and yoghurt—and cream? They all come from animals.'

'Not *dead* animals though.'

'Eggs are dead.'

Caroline thought. 'But they've never been alive. Heck, we've got to eat *something*, Sarah: we'll get ill otherwise.'

'Some people don't eat anything like that,' Sarah insisted. 'I've read about them. They're called vegans.'

'What *do* they eat then?'

'Bread and lentils and rice and nuts and things.'

'Lentils? Yuck!'

'But they have to take vitamin pills, or they waste away and die.'

'Look,' said Caroline firmly, 'I think we should carry on eating milk and eggs and things like that. We don't want to get ill. We couldn't help the animals if

46

we did. It can't be cruel to milk a cow, can it?'

'I'm not sure,' said Sarah. 'Don't they get strapped up to horrible big milking machines? It can't be much fun.'

'But if they weren't milked, their udders would burst and they'd die, wouldn't they?'

'Only because the farmers take their calves away from them,' said Sarah. 'It's the calves who are supposed to have the milk really. It's exactly the same as snatching a new-born baby away from its mother. If that's not cruel, I don't know what is.'

They sat in silence, pondering this for a while.

'One step at a time,' said Caroline at last. 'Mum'll freak out if we present her with a huge list of things we won't eat, all at once. We ought to be reasonable about it. How about giving up meat first, then we'll think about milk, etc later. That way we can get used to it gradually.'

'OK,' said Sarah. She thought some more. 'What about Aslan though? Cat food's mostly meat, isn't it?'

Caroline stroked him fondly. 'We'll think about that. We don't want his lordship to suffer at all, do we—eh, Puss, Puss? He's an animal too, don't forget!'

Sarah stifled a pang of disappointment. Now it seemed like Caz who was being defeatist. Oh well.

'We'd better go and break the news to Mum,' she said.

They went downstairs. Mum was in the kitchen, busy chopping onions and pork into slivers for the evening meal.

'Hello, girls,' she said absent-mindedly. 'I thought we'd have a Chinese stir-fry for a change.'

Sarah and Caroline looked at the meat and then at each other.

'Why don't you put something else in it, instead of meat?' said Caroline brightly.

'Well . . . like what? Go on, Caz, give me some ideas.'

'Egg,' said Caroline. 'Don't they have something Chinesey with egg called *foo-yung* or something?'

'What? Oh yes, maybe. We could try that next time. Strips of omelette, I think it is.'

'Or nuts,' said Sarah, 'or seeds. Or things made with soya beans.'

'Not sure I fancy that,' said Mum. She scooped the completed plateful of pale meat slivers into a bowl, consulted her recipe book and tipped a generous helping of soy sauce and spices over it. 'Now—I'll leave that to stand for an hour or so. What's up with you two anyway? Haven't you got any homework? Looking for a job to do? You can . . .'

'Mum,' said Sarah, 'we want to tell you something.'

Mum sat down and put on her serious, concerned expression. 'Go on then, loves.'

Caroline opened her mouth.

'*I'll* say it,' said Sarah. 'We've decided to go vegetarian.'

Mum smiled indulgently. It wasn't an unkind smile, but a sort of patronizing one, that they both remembered from as far back as toddler days. It always made their hackles rise.

'Don't laugh!' said Caroline fiercely.

'I'm not laughing,' cried Mum indignantly. 'Come on then, you'd better tell me more, all the whys and wherefores. Is this some idea you've picked up at your new school or something?'

'No,' said Sarah, 'we've worked it out ourselves.'

'I see. But . . . may I ask why?'

'We don't believe in hurting or killing animals,' said Sarah. Mum smiled again, so she added, 'And it's not a passing phase, we won't grow out of it.'

'I could say I've heard that before,' said Mum, 'but I won't. Well then, OK, no meat. What about fish?'

They looked at each other. 'We haven't decided about that yet,' said Caroline.

Mum nodded. 'Eggs? Oh, you've already suggested them for dinner, so they must be all right. Milk and cheese?'

They nodded.

'Hmm,' said Mum, 'that's not so bad then. I suppose we could get into nut patés and buckwheat roasts and things as well. I don't mind that too much. You know I like trying new recipes. I quite fancy getting myself a vegetarian cookbook actually.'

They breathed a sigh of relief.

'But so long as you don't expect Dad and me to give up meat too?'

'We've got no choice I suppose,' said Caroline.

'You could always follow our good example,' said Sarah.

'*I* wouldn't mind that much of course,' said Mum loftily, 'but can you imagine Dad? "Wot, no meat?!"' She mimicked the adverts they'd all laughed at in the butcher's shop. 'But you don't intend to start straight away, do you? I hope—surely you can manage to eat one last helping of meat tonight? *Please*. It would be such a bore at this late stage to have to do something separate for you.'

'We could get our own dinner,' said Sarah.

'Don't be so silly! From tomorrow I'll do something that you like, I promise.'

'We could just eat the onions and rice,' said Caroline.

'You will not! You're growing girls: you need the protein.'

'Oh, all right then,' said Caroline placatingly.

Sarah shot her a cross look.

At supper time, Dad was in a hearty mood.

'Spent the afternoon having a chat with the local landowner,' he said. 'Sir Hugh Something-man.'

'Harryman,' said Sarah.'

'That's it. Quite a nice chap. Bit eccentric, but nothing uppity about him. He was telling me all about the shoots he has on his estate. Pheasant and grouse, mainly. Brings in thousands of pounds, apparently. Gets MPs and all sorts of other what-nots coming up from London, just for the sport.'

He stuck a fork into his dinner. 'Mmm, this is good! What is it?'

'It's from that Chinese cookery course on TV,' said Mum.

'I like it, I like it! Hey, what's up, Sarah? Aren't you hungry?'

'I feel sick,' said Sarah quietly.

Dad looked concerned. 'Got a bug?'

She shook her head. Caroline's plate was clean, Mum and Dad were both on second helpings. Tears welled up in her eyes.

'I can't . . . can't eat it.'

'What's up, love?' Dad was all concerned.

'She doesn't like the meat.' Mum explained.

'We're both going vegetarian as from tomorrow,' said Caroline.

Dad's eyebrows shot up comically. If he was going

to make a joke of it ... The tears welled over and began to trickle down Sarah's cheeks. But it wasn't just the meat business ... it was everything: secrets and sneaking out and pretending. She hated deceit and now she was deceiving everyone: Mum, Dad, Caz, Ian ...

She got up and fled from the room. Caroline came after her.

'Sarah—you know what Dad's like. You shouldn't let him ...'

'It isn't that.' Sarah turned to face her sister. It all seemed so impossible. 'We'll never live up to it.'

'What?'

'I mean, we'll always hurt animals. Every day. I swotted a fly today. I drowned a spider in the bath. I ...'

'Sarah, they're not animals, they're insects.'

They went into Sarah's bedroom and closed the door. Aslan was still lounging hopefully on the bed. Sarah picked him up and let her tears pour into his soft fur. She pulled a handful of tissues from the box lying untidily on the floor and blew her nose loudly.

'Did you know they've put mouse poison in the pantry?' she said at last.

'Have they?' said Caroline. They sat down side by side on the bed and Caroline put an arm round her sister. Sarah sobbed loudly, letting Caz comfort her for a few monents; but it was no good: she was deceiving *her* too.

'... dreadful,' Caroline was saying. 'We can't poison animals in our own house. We'll have to get rid of it.'

'But you know how Mum's dead scared—round the twist—about mice,' said Sarah. 'And Dad says they spread disease. Anyway, what can we do with the poison? It's deadly. We can't just dump it in the dustbin. Supposing Aslan got hold of it—or a little mouse could probably just as well get it in there.'

'But fancy slaughtering things in our own house!' cried Caroline. 'Our own mother and father! We'll have to educate them.'

'I suppose they mean it for the best,' said Sarah. 'They just don't think it through like we do. Anyway, look at me, killing insects.' She blew her nose, then burst into tears again. 'Oh, and another thing I've been thinking about Caz: leather.'

'Leather? Oh, Sarah, yes—the skin of dead animals!'

'So—oughtn't we to stop wearing leather shoes?'

Caroline thought.

'Some leather things are made from animals that are dead already,' she said. 'I mean, they don't have to specially kill them, do they, like for meat. Perhaps it's not as bad . . .'

The door clicked open suddenly.

'Look loves,' said Dad, 'Sarah—Mum's explained about it. I wasn't going to laugh at you, honestly. I think your feelings about animals are very admirable.' He shoved his hands in his pockets awkwardly. 'I just don't want you to go getting too extreme about it, that's all.'

'You've been listening at the door!' Caroline challenged him.

'Caroline! What a thing to say to your fa . . .'

'You've been poisoning mice!' cried Sarah.

'What? Oh yes, that. You noticed did you? We weren't going to mention it to you actually. Thought you might be a bit put off at the idea of mice running round the house.'

They both snorted contemptuously.

'But that's murder!'

'Oh, Sarah, for crying out loud! Mice are—they're filthy vermin! Look, if you insist, I'll show you what they do. Come on!'

He grabbed the girls each by the wrist and pulled them along, back through the kitchen, to the large, walk-in pantry. Mum, busy with clearing away, pretended to take no notice.

'Look! Your mother had fifty fits when she found this.'

Three large, unopened packets of flour were piled neatly on a shelf. The bottom two each had a large hole chewed through the corner: flour spilled out from them all along the shelf, mixed with a thick scattering of small, dark mouse droppings. They gave off a sickly-stale animal smell. Nearby, in the vegetable rack, three carrots had been pulled out and were covered in tiny gnawings and tooth marks. There were more droppings trailed randomly across the floor.

'In mediaeval times, this sort of thing spread the Plague,' said Dad. 'It's foul! We'd all go down ill like nine-pins if we didn't get rid of the wretched things.'

'Couldn't you have set Aslan to catch them?' said Caroline tightly.

'That lazy, over-fed animal! He's never caught anything in his life.'

'No,' cried Sarah, 'because he's kind and gentle like us!'

'Anyway, what's the difference to a mouse whether it's killed by a cat or by humans, eh?'

'At least it's *natural* for a cat to catch mice,' said Sarah, 'instinct. Not like . . .'

'Oh! Then it's a natural instinct for people to eat meat!' Dad was shouting now. 'Listen, you two, I'd like to be calm about this vegetarian business, but hearing your ideas, you just sound like a couple of real fruit-and-nut cases! Oh, you've got all these high falutin' moral principles, but what do you really know about the world, eh?

'I tell you, you'd never eat *anything* if you thought about it too much . . . You'd never even eat baked beans if you had any idea how the cans they come in are made, exploiting child labour in the Third World tin mines, polluting the environment . . .'

Chapter Six

It was different, this time, creeping out at night.

Firstly, she was alone.

Aloneness was good in a way: it felt free, exhilarating, close to the wild ones ... An owl hooted and a long way off, a roe deer barked. She turned her torch off and padded along in the blue darkness for a while, feeling like a dark blue molecule herself, at one with the night.

Secondly, she was walking steadily along a road, instead of stumbling up an overgrown foot-path.

In some ways, that made things easier: there was nothing to trip over, no chance of losing the way. Nevertheless, there were real dangers: for the occasional passing car could easily spot her in its headlights. She was terrified of attackers; or, on a different level, worried that a local farmer or villager might recognize her and insist on ferrying her straight home.

So whenever she heard a car approaching, she jumped quickly, quietly into the shadows of a ditch that ran below the hedge, crouching there until the blinding lights and the engine roar had passed.

That made her feel close to the wild ones too. She thought of all the small, unknown creatures that must be cowering anonymously alongside her: shrews, voles, hedgehogs, field mice, rabbits, all sheltering from the pitiless menace of modern humankind.

Ian had told her the quick way into the badger wood: through a swing-gate, then straight down a broad track, soft with beech-mast. Stop where it peters out, he had said, turn out your light, give a low whistle, then wait.

She found the place, whistled, waited.

Almost at once, quiet footfalls came, growing closer: then a dark shape separated itself from the night shadows and the trees.

'Stone me!' whispered Ian, 'you actually came!'

'Of course I did. I said I would.'

'Shh! Not so loud. You haven't got a torch on or anything? Good. Now, come with me, just follow where I lead, don't say *anything*. We mustn't make a sound while we're near the sett. Try not to crackle any twigs.'

He took her hand in a cold, limp grip. His own hand felt calloused and scarred: the marks of tooth, claw and beak from the animals he nursed, so she guessed, like the hands of a seasoned vet. She felt a pang of envy.

'OK?' he whispered.

'OK.'

They set off into the woods. At the clearing where the sett was, Ian pushed her silently against a tree, pinning her back with a long, gangly arm. For a moment she felt threatened and tried to break free; then suddenly she saw what he was watching, and at once her senses tightened to vivid alertness.

Dark against dark, the white stripes of its face standing out startlingly, a badger came shuffling out from the earth.

56

It was bigger than she'd expected. It moved with a kind of lumbering majesty, rooting here, there, pausing every few seconds to sniff the still night air.

Suddenly it stopped, its nose twitching towards them. Ian's arm stiffened, and she stiffened with it.

The badger hesitated, sniffed again—and then turned hastily back, disappearing into the shadows.

'Shucks,' sighed Ian, 'it's smelt us. Come on. There's no point in hanging around.'

He took her hand again and steered her firmly back the way that they had come.

'Is it my fault?' she whispered.

'Well, maybe you pong more than me! No, it happens sometimes, specially on still nights when it's impossible to get down-wind because there isn't any wind.'

'And that's it? It won't come back? We won't see any more?'

'Not tonight,' said Ian cheerfully, speaking at an almost normal pitch now. 'Never mind. There's always tomorrow.'

'I can't keep on sneaking out like this,' said Sarah. 'They'll find me out.'

They'd reached the gate now: beyond it lay the road and their opposite paths. Ian pulled a small kit-bag out from its hiding place in the dead bracken by the fence and offered her a steaming drink of hot chocolate from his flask.

'But why do you have to *sneak* out?' he asked, sounding really surprised. 'Don't your folk approve of things like badger watching?'

Sarah thought. It had never even occurred to her to ask Mum and Dad's permission to come out tonight. She supposed that was because it had seemed like a

57

natural extension of her secret midnight campaign with Caz, and guilt about the one had rubbed off onto the other.

She'd always hated keeping secrets from anyone; so however had she got herself tangled now in such a web of unnecessary deceit?

'I . . . I don't know,' she said truthfully. 'I suppose it's my sister really. She's funny about things. She'd hate it if I went out on something like this without her.'

'What the hell's up with her?' asked Ian. 'She seems a real weirdo.'

Sarah shrugged in the darkness. 'I can't explain.'

Ian offered her another swig from his flask. '*You're* all right though,' he said. He paused, and she sensed his awkwardness.

'Hey, Sarah,' he burst out, 'listen, I was wondering if you'd, um, do something for me. I mean, like, *with* me.'

'Well! Like what?'

'I want you to help me catch these anarchists. You know, the vandals. The ones going round wrecking my dad's traps.'

'What?' Cold panic swept through her. 'What do you mean?' Yet she was surprised at how steady her voice sounded.

'My old man's far too defeatist about it,' said Ian. 'He reckons he'll never catch them, that it's just some daft louts up from Leeds or Bradford or somewhere, just a passing phase.'

'Well, maybe he's right,' she said carefully.

'He's not, I reckon,' said Ian. 'It's like the poachers. They come out, week after week, and then they stop for a while and you think, good, they've been scared off—and then they start up again.'

'But so what?' said Sarah. 'It's your dad's worry, isn't it, not yours. It's his job, after all. He must know what he's doing.'

'It really bugs me,' said Ian. He clicked the cap onto his flask, stuffed it back inside the kit-bag and leaned over the gate. 'Dad's too nice, too soft. These vandals are so . . . so ignorant—they're useless! They don't have any idea what it's about, looking after a big estate. They think, oh, free a few animals and the world's OK. They don't understand the delicate balance.

'What my dad does is all for *conservation*, honest. You know, that naturalist lot, they're always going on about how important it is to have thick hedgerows and proper woods with beech trees and oaks and things? Well, all the hedges and woods around here are only kept that way so that the pheasants can live in them: it's my dad who looks after them—it's thanks to him that there's so much wildlife! And then just 'cause he has to get rid of a few foxes and things because he protects them so well that there's too many of them, these . . . these . . .'

He pounded the gate angrily with his fist.

'It makes me right *mad*, I tell you, Sarah, these filthy so-and-sos, driving out here with their city ideas, trying to force their ignorance onto my hills!'

'*Your* hills?' She was desperately playing for time: her mind was reeling.

Through the shadows, Ian met her eye. 'They feel that way, Sarah. I've grown up with them, see, walked on them a lot by myself since I was little. I won't have outsiders mucking things up.'

He unlatched the gate and started to swing on it.

59

'So—you gonna help me?'

'I . . . I don't know. I don't understand enough about it.' In a panic, she almost gave herself away. 'Ian, I don't know whether I even agree with you about foxes and things. Maybe—don't forget I haven't lived here very long—I mean, it seems so awful to trap them. Anyway, why do you want *me* to help you with this? There must be loads of other . . .'

'But you've told me!' cried Ian, 'you said you care about animals like I do! For goodness' sake, Sarah, you don't want to see the balance of things in the country, the way things have always been for years— for centuries—ruined, do you?'

There was a logic she couldn't quite follow in his argument, an echo of Caroline's own brand of passion which unnerved her.

'Of course not! But *because* I care about animals . . .'

'Well then! And you live right nearby—' he swung the gate towards her 'you know, nearby where these louts struck last time. The snares they smashed up are just up the hill from your house. There's even a path leads towards them. You're at the sharp end, like.'

'Oh!' Sarah swallowed. 'I hadn't realized it was quite so close.' She was glad it was night: if Ian could see her flushing, surely he would guess the truth. She was cornered. Her thoughts darted about, pin-pricks of cunning lighting the dark sea of her panic.

'I wouldn't normally ask this sort of thing of a girl, of course, but like I said, you seem all right. All I want you to do is keep a good look-out. When you're at home, specially after dark. I want you to watch out for folk going up and down the footpath by your house. Can't be that many—not now, outside the holiday season. Well, there could be a few ramblers and things . . . Anyway, if you could get car numbers and descriptions of the people—all of them, like, even the ones who don't look suspicious.'

He slipped off the gate and hitched the kit-bag over his shoulder.

'See, often it's the ones who look most innocent that are really guilty. That's what Dad always says about poachers. What I thought was, we'd do a bit of private detective work, like you and me. Then when we've got some really good clues and information, we'll pass it on to my old man, and he can pass it to the police.'

It was all so beautifully simple. She had a feeling there must be a simple way out of it too, but in the chill night air she couldn't put her finger on it.

'But I can't keep going outside to spy on the footpath,' she said lamely. 'My people will wonder what on earth I'm up to—they'll think I've gone mad!'

'Well, why the hell don't you tell them?' exclaimed Ian. 'Your mum and dad are on the side of law and order, aren't they—even if your daft sister's a pain up the backside? There's nothing wrong in trying to catch criminals, heh? I mean, I tell my dad almost everything.'

'You don't understand,' said Sarah sadly. She wanted to cry. She felt she was being torn apart. *This isn't me, it isn't!* She shook herself like a dog. 'Look, I'm getting cold, Ian—I'd best go home.'

He held the gate open for her and watched silently while she passed through it.

'Anyway, thanks ever so much,' said Sarah, keeping her voice steady. 'It was fantastic seeing the badger, even though it wasn't for long.' She managed to grin to herself, imagining how Caz would envy her if she ever found out.

'It's all right,'muttered Ian.

'And listen,' she added on an impulse,'I . . . I'll try to help you. But I can't promise very much. I mean, I can keep a look-out for you sometimes.' After all, she had nothing to lose or give away by doing that.

Through her despair, she began to see the humour of her situation: wasn't this what they called being a double-agent?

She would decide when she was ready, whether to commit herself properly to Caz—or maybe even to Ian. Meanwhile, she would listen carefully to what both had to say, she would learn as much as she could, and follow her own nose, while trying to work out what was really best for the animals.

Dangerous game, crazy game: in the cold night air, she heard the owl hoot again and, a long way off, a sudden blood-curdling shriek.

'Sounds like something has just caught its dinner,' said Ian.

Or got snared? wondered Sarah silently.

As if he could read her thoughts, Ian shook his head and flashed her an unconvincing smile. Then he turned abruptly and slipped off into the woods.

Chapter Seven

This time, Caroline and Sarah went out on their animal rescue mission in broad daylight. They told Mum they were going for a picnic on the hills.

'It's lovely to see you enjoying the countryside so much.' She was completely taken in by their apparent innocence. Caroline grinned, and Sarah envied her nonchalance, feeling more wretched than ever.

Mum gave them cold pizzas to eat, and a small container full of garden raspberries from the freezer.

'Just you stick to the footpaths though,' she said, 'and remember—don't go talking to any strangers you meet—don't even go near them.'

'Mum,' said Caroline, 'this isn't Leeds! No one goes up on the hills.'

'No, well, there might be peculiar people out walking. I don't have to remind you of the awful things that can happen to girls—anywhere. They say there's poachers around—nasty characters they're supposed to be—Caz, I'm serious about this, mind. And there's those weirdo animal liberationist people who've been going around vandalizing the gamekeeper's equipment—everyone was talking about it at the Women's Institute meeting last night.'

'Oh,' said Caroline brazenly, 'if we meet *them* we'll congratulate them and ask if we can join the cause!'

'Caroline Carr!' Mum was horrified.

'She's only joking,' said Sarah quickly. 'Anyway, you wouldn't get people like that out in broad daylight on a sunny Saturday, would you?'

'Well, just you take care anyway.'

They ambled slowly up the footpath opposite their cottage, trying to look leisurely and normal.

'Fancy you saying that to Mum!' said Sarah.

'Saying what?'

'About joining the animal liberationists.'

Caroline laughed. 'Well, why not? She needs to be shocked sometimes—she's so respectable. Anyway, Mum of all people would never ever guess it was us.'

'How can you be so sure?'

'Mothers never think badly of their children.'

'Maybe not,' said Sarah slowly, 'but I don't like deceiving people. Specially my own family.' Her hands were clenched, the nails driving into the palms. 'In fact, I *hate* it!'

Caroline stopped and took Sarah's arm in her long, slim fingers.

'You're making me feel bad about dragging you into this again, little sister,' she said. 'Please tell me, Sarah—now. *Do* you want to go on with the rescue mission or not? The last thing I want is to force you into it.'

Here's your chance, thought Sarah. She could end it now, if she wanted to, with a few honest words. She toyed with the idea wistfully.

Caroline was searching her face intently. Sarah took a deep breath.

'Look, let's sit down a minute,' said Caroline. 'There's no hurry.'

She led Sarah off the path, down to the beck. They

found a place to sit on some boulders cushioned with soft, damp moss. The water tumbled past them, clear and tranquil, gushing peaty-brown and silver over the stones. They watched it for a while; but their silence wasn't companionable.

At last Caroline said, 'So—you don't really want to be part of this any more, do you?'

'I never said that.'

'No-o.' Caroline pulled up a frond of moss and began tearing it neatly into shreds. 'But I can tell. You're always humming and haaing about it, making excuses.'

'That's not true! I've come with you today!'

'Yes. But you made me delay it from the other night. If you *really* cared about the animals . . .'

First Ian, now Caz—how could they question whether she loved the animls? If there was one thing she was absolutely certain about, it was that.

'You keep making out that I don't care—but *I* was the one who suggested giving up meat!'

'Mmm.'

'Wasn't I?'

'Yes, yes, of course you were, Sarah. But still . . . you're not that keen on the rescue mission, are you?'

Sarah sighed. 'Look, I'm scared of getting caught. What we're doing, it's probably—I'm sure it is— against the law. We could get sent to one of these approved schools or whatever they're called, locked up with a load of *real* baddies! Imagine it Caz!'

'We won't let ourselves get caught,' said Caroline fiercely.

There was another silence. The flow of the beck drummed in Sarah's ears.

'OK then,' she said softly, 'you're right Caz. I'm

not at all sure about this whole business.'

'There! I knew it! It's because you've been talking to people at school!'

'Of course I have! I want to make friends, don't I? You didn't lose much time getting thick with Emma and that other girl, what's-her-name? It's hard enough, isn't it, moving and changing schools: on top of that, now you're trying to turn me into an outcast!' Tears pricked at her eyes, but she forced them back, determined not to give Caz the satisfaction of seeing her cry.

'Just calm down,' said Caroline sweetly. 'Of course you need friends. All I'm saying is, can't you keep away from . . . oh, you know what I mean, the wrong sort: like that wimp of a gamekeeper's son.'

'Wrong sort?!' mimicked Sarah. 'Listen to yourself, Caz, you snob! And Ian's not a wimp—he's a good bloke. He's in my class and we're neighbours—why shouldn't I talk to him?'

'He's your boyfriend.'

'My *what?*! Caz, you know I'm not interested in boys. Not like that. Not like you and your cronies. I've seen the three of you at school, preening yourselves and . . .'

'People are gossiping about you and him, you know,' said Caroline spitefully.

'You must be joking! Even if I was interested in boys in that way, it certainly wouldn't be in someone like him! I mean, pop stars are OK and that sort of thing . . .'

She couldn't believe it, *didn't* believe it was true. She knew it was just Caz's nastiest, most cunning way of trying to win her over. And yet . . . if there *was* a grain of truth in it . . . She felt hot with embarrassment.

Supposing Ian saw it that way? She'd always talked to boys quite a bit: Caz had never been snide about it before. She's baiting you, said the little voice inside her head. Best thing, shrug it off.

Sarah took a deep breath. 'Anyway,' she said evenly, '*everyone's* talking about animals and the game-keeper thing.'

'And of course, you follow the safest tide of opinion,' accused Caroline, 'like a silly little sheep!'

'There isn't a tide of opinion—not in my class, anyway. Everyone's arguing about it from both sides. But at least I do listen to other points of view—unlike someone else I know!'

'Other people's points of view! It's just brainwashing!'

'If anyone's trying to brainwash me, it's *you,*' Sarah threw back at her. 'But anyway, about this thing of trapping—lots of people say foxes and weasels and stoats and that are awful vermin—pests.'

'People say! It's only the gamekeepers.'

'No, lots of other people too,' said Sarah. 'Apparently the farmers hate them. If a fox gets into a henhouse, it can cause havoc—it's supposed to be horrible; and also they sometimes attack new-born lambs. They're animals too, you know.'

'Farmers!' snorted Caroline. 'They keep most of the poor chickens locked up in battery units—torture chambers. The foxes couldn't get them there.'

'That's not true,' said Sarah. 'At least four people in my class who live on farms keep free-range chickens. Honestly. And they've all been attacked by foxes at some time. Apparently they kill the lot all in one go—but then maybe they'll only bother to carry one away

67

to actually eat it. See, they're just as brutal as humans.'

Caroline sat motionless, staring at the beck through her silky curtain of hair. Sarah could see her lips working silently on a knowing reply. But the retort didn't come. Instead, she tossed her head suddenly, stood up, and said in her brightest voice:

'Oh, all this pointless talk! What does it matter what other people say or think? The animals are waiting for us to help them—and here we are, just wasting the day!'

She clambered quickly back up the bank and set off up the path, pausing to give Sarah one of her familiar big-sister grins of encouragement.

Sarah hesitated; but following Caz was a habit.

'OK, I'll come with you today, but . . .'

'That's great!'

'. . . but afterwards I need to think things through some more.'

'We'll talk things through together,' promised Caroline. 'I'll show you some of the books I've read up—most of them are quite easy to understand—and some of the campaign leaflets I sent off for, then you'll realize what it's all about a bit better. Look, I swear to you, what we're doing: there's nothing wrong with it. Even if we are maybe breaking the law, it's absolutely for the good—like Robin Hood—being outlaws to stop suffering. Don't you see?'

She waited for Sarah to catch her up and linked arms with her. 'Now come on, stop worrying.'

Sarah hadn't been up the hill since that vivid night a couple of weeks ago. It seemed quite different in daylight: less threatening, just huge and beautiful. Behind them, sheep-cropped grass sloped down to the road. Ahead, the hill rose, clumped with bracken and heather, to distant zig-zags of dry-stone walls, and thick plantations of woodland.

Beyond the next fold, a pair of birds rose suddenly from the heather with a loud drumming of wings, calling *lek-lek-lek*.

'Grouse,' said Caroline. 'That's some of what they shoot. That's what the trapping's all about.'

Sarah stared after them. 'It hardly seems worth it,' she said. 'They look so small.'

'I know,' said Caroline,' 'and they end up full of lead bullets from the guns! Crazy, isn't it?'

They crossed the beck and came to the gate marked *keep out*. This time they put on gloves to climb over it.

The woods beyond it were green and cool. Sarah's stomach tightened as they crept across the soft brown carpet of leaves and pine needles under the trees.

'The first snare's down there,' said Caroline. 'Wait here. I'll go and see if there's anything in it.'

She ran into the trees.

'Sarah!' Her voice was half-way between a yelp and a whisper. 'It's . . . There's a fox!'

Excitement welled up in Sarah, threatening to choke her. She forgot how she'd argued just now that foxes were vermin. A wild one, needing help! Breathless, she ran to see.

The fox was a young one, the colour of red-brown autumn leaves. It was caught in the snare by its front leg: as it had struggled hopelessly to free itself, the wire had tightened and cut through deep into its flesh. Blood had congealed thickly round the wound. Still struggling, it snarled and whimpered, snarled and whimpered, like a bad-tempered dog. As Sarah approached, it bared its teeth at them, then collapsed suddenly in a stupor of pain.

Caroline wielded her wire cutters bravely, but the fox roused itself, twisted round and tried to snap at her.

'Stop it, stop it!' she shrieked. 'Oh, you stupid thing, I'm trying to help you, not hurt you!'

'He doesn't know that,' said Sarah breathlessly. 'How can he? He couldn't dream of trusting anyone human! We ought to try soothing him first. Think of what Aslan likes: soft words, smoochy noises.'

She crouched as close as she dared and offered her open hand just beyond the fox's reach, in a gesture which she hoped it might interpret as friendship. 'Here, boy.' Her voice was hoarse and gentle. 'It's all right, all right. We won't hurt you. Shh, shh, there, there.'

The fox watched her suspiciously, still snarling.

'I bet he thinks you're shamming,' said Caroline. 'I just don't know how we're going to do this. He's so big, so much stronger than the stoat.'

Ideas flashed through Sarah's mind. 'Maybe if we distract him so that he can't see what we're doing—if we throw a jacket over him or something . . .?'

'But then he'd struggle even more.'

'Yes . . . But if he can't see it might take his mind off his poor leg while you . . . I mean, it would only take a second or two to free it.'

'OK,' said Caroline, 'we'll try.'

They were both trembling now. Sarah pulled off her parka and threw it. It landed square over the fox's head. For a few moments it jerked wildly while the fox struggled; then suddenly stopped dead still. In that instant, Caroline lunged forward with the cutters.

'I can't get to the wire . . . Ah, that's it—oh! Oh no, Sarah, I think I cut his leg too . . . Quick, get *back!*'

Sarah jumped away just in time. With a new burst of energy, the fox shook itself so violently that the parka fell away.

Now it began to worry and drag at the snared leg again—and found to its amazement that it was free. They saw its eyes flare with a mixture of emotions they could only guess at.

The girls hesitated, half cowering against the trees, ready to run if it should turn on them. But its sole interest was escape. It sprang forward—collapsed on its injured leg that was pouring blood again—and gave a whine of fury and pain.

'Oh how awful!' Caroline pointed to the wound. Under the fresh blood, matted fur and torn skin hung from it in shreds. A handful of flies was already starting to colonize it. 'We must do something for him. I wonder how long he's been here.'

'Hours and hours,' said Sarah bleakly. 'He must have lost a lot of blood. He must be starving.'

'Perhaps he'll die anyway,' said Caroline. 'Perhaps this has just been a waste of time.'

'No! We've *got* to save him!'

They looked at each other uncertainly.

'We could try to make a sort of stretcher,' said Caroline.

'Yes—out of sticks and branches. We could bundle him up in our parkas so he can't struggle and carry him to safety.'

Caroline ruefully patted the plaster she still wore on her stoat bite. 'But I don't want any more injuries. Perhaps we could get someone to look at him. If only there were someone we knew we could trust: a vet, or someone from the Naturalists' Trust . . .'

Or Ian, thought Sarah recklessly. She wouldn't dare—or would she? After all, when you were a double-agent, everything you did was a calculated risk.

'I know someone who might possibly help,' she said.

'Good on you! Who is it? Sarah, for goodness sake, it mustn't be anyone who'd suspect what we've done.'

'I know. That's the trouble. It could be . . . a bit risky. Let me think about it while we get the poor thing trussed up.'

The fox had given up licking its wound. It lay panting, scarcely moving, watching them through dull eyes.

They set to work gathering strong fallen branches and lashing them together with fronds of grass and bracken. Within ten minutes they had a rough, make-shift stretcher.

'Not bad, eh?' said Sarah.

'Mmm. We need to practise more at making things like this. It's a vital skill for our mission.'

Grimy and sweating, they grinned openly at each other for the first time in days. Caroline squeezed Sarah's hand.

'We're a good team. Come on, let's see to our friend.'

Now the fox was half dozing, half unconscious. They tied their jackets carefully together by the hoods and sleeves to make a sort of sack, crept up to the fox, threw the sack across, rolled it over quickly and tied it shut. There were enough holes and gaps for the air to get in. Caroline pulled the belt from her jeans and used it to strap the bundled fox into place on the stretcher. It twitched a bit, but scarcely protested.

'I'll go in front,' said Caroline.

They lifted an end each and set off down the track.

'Awf! I never expected him to be this heavy!' panted Sarah.

'You OK?' Caroline tried to look back over her shoulder, but the stretcher got in the way.

'I think so. Just hope the stretcher doesn't collapse.'

'And that Fox is all right!'

'Yes—he's very still.'

'But we can't keep stopping to check him.'

At the gate they achieved a remarkable feat of pushing and shoving to get the loaded stretcher over the top. On the other side, they rested for a few moments. The fox lay inert inside the bundle.

'He's not . . . dead is he?' said Sarah. 'We don't want to hump him all this way for nothing.'

'Shh.' Pause. 'No, he's breathing. For goodness' sake, we mustn't give up now!'

Sarah sighed. 'Come on then.'

They hoisted up their burden again and began to pick their way down the path.

'I hope no one sees us here,' puffed Caroline. 'Let's think: when we get to the bottom, we'll have to hide him somewhere for a while.'

'There's a load of thick bracken by the gate,' suggested Sarah. 'If we leave him well off the path, even if anyone's out walking, they probably won't see him.'

'Good idea. Meanwhile, we mustn't waste any time working out what to do.'

'Right.'

'So—have you decided—can you tell me about this, er, person you said could possibly help?'

'Oh!' Sarah was caught unawares. 'Let me just think a bit more. I'm not too sure whether he would be safe.'

They reached the bottom of the hill and set the stretcher down. The bracken that grew here was dead and dry, but almost shoulder-high. They tunnelled into it and beat down a cavernous hide-out. Then they loosened the fox and rolled it gently off the stretcher, out of its wrappings and onto the soft earth. It opened its eyes and bared its teeth at them, weakly, hopelessly.

'Do you think he'll be all right here?' asked Sarah.

Caroline shrugged. 'Let's hope so. But he must be starving. What do foxes eat?'

'Grouse and pheasants,' said Sarah flatly. 'Chickens. Rabbits.'

'Oh gawd! We'll have to think about this one. Come on, let's go home and clean up a bit. Then we'll go for a vet or something.'

They went through the gate and crossed the road to their cottage.

'Oh,' said Caroline, 'we never ate Mum's lovely pizza, or the raspberries. He could have the . . . Sarah, what's the matter?'

For Sarah had turned ghostly-pale. She pointed a trembling finger towards the drive-way of their cottage.

'There's a strange car there,' said Caroline matter of factly. 'Someone's visiting. Now who . . .? I'm sure I've seen that car before. Lots of times.'

'You have,' said Sarah.

'Do you know who it is then?'

'Yes.' Sarah struggled to stop her voice from breaking into a frightened sob. 'It's Mr Metcalfe.'

'Metcalfe? Oh, I know . . .!'

'Yes, the *gamekeeper* of all people! And look at us, Caz, just look—we've both got fox blood all over our clothes!'

Chapter Eight

'We don't have to go home yet,' said Sarah weakly.

'I think we should,' said Caroline. 'We'd better try and find out what old Metcalfe is up to and whether it's anything to worry about. We might be able to get away without actually meeting him.'

She led the way up the drive. The front door was half ajar and good-humoured voices were drifting out of the lounge. They crept in, dashed for their bedrooms and changed their blood-stained clothes as fast as they could. In the bathroom they bumped against each other, scrubbing the dirt and blood off their hands and arms.

'This is what murderers must do,' said Sarah.

'Don't be so morbid!' Caroline was matter of fact. 'We're saving life, not killing it. Now, you look fine, really innocent. Are you ready?'

'Ye-es. OK.'

They hovered outside the lounge door, trying to make out the conversation. Mr Metcalfe's voice boomed cheerfully above their father's. Suddenly there was a pause, then footsteps. Before they could flee, the door opened.

'Hello, girls!' said Mum. 'Back already? I thought I heard something. Come in and meet Mr Metcalfe. These are our girls: Caroline and Sarah.'

'Aye well, I've met Sarah already of course. Over at our place only the other day.' He winked at her. 'Examining our Ian's collection of sick animals, eh? How yer doing then, lass?'

Sarah stared at the floor. She could feel Caz's disbelieving fury burning into her. Mum and Dad were watching her with curious interest. They were all waiting for her to speak.

'All right,' she whispered.

Caz's anger stabbed at her like little arrow pricks: *deceit, deceit.*

'Well,' grinned Dad, 'just goes to show, we're always the last ones to be introduced! Anyway, we must show the girls—'

'Yes!' said Mum. Sarah noticed that she was flushed with excitement. 'Mr Metcalfe's brought us a brace of pheasant! Isn't that kind!'

She held the gift up to show them: a cock and a hen pheasant hooked together, lifeless but still fully resplendent in their beautiful plumage.

Dead meat, dead flesh, thought Sarah bleakly. There was something indecent in their parents' pleasure over it.

'Now now, it's not me that's kind,' said Mr Metcalfe. 'All I did was to deliver it—compliments of the estate, it is. It's Sir Hugh you want to thank really.'

'Oh, you can be sure we will,' said Mum with real feeling.

'Ever tasted pheasant before, girls?' asked Mr Metcalfe conversationally.

'Er—no,' said Sarah carefully. She gritted her teeth, praying without hope that her sister would not embarrass her.

Sure enough, Caroline announced loud and clear:

'We don't eat meat.' She looked the gamekeeper directly, coldly in the eye. 'We're vegetarians. We think it's wrong to kill animals and birds.'

Mr Metcalfe's eyebrows shot up. 'Oh! You should have told me. I'm sorry—then it's really an unwelcome gift.'

'No no, not *us*,' said Dad hastily. 'Janet and I are truly delighted, I promise you. It's only these two whacky daughters of ours who have suddenly developed these, er, eccentric ideas. It just means there's all the more for us.'

Mr Metcalfe smiled, but he was clearly taken aback.

'Ah!' he said suddenly, 'I almost forgot! There's something else I'm supposed to bring you, as well as the birds. An invitation. Sir Hugh' (he cleared his throat grandly) '. . . requests the honour of your presence at one of his shooting parties.'

'I say!' exclaimed Dad. 'Some of my old colleagues in Leeds would have given anything to be invited to a shoot. Now we really have arrived!'

'Both of us?' asked Mum.

Mr Metcalfe nodded. 'Aye. There's ladies come too—if you fancy it. But you'll need all the gear: thick sweater, a windproof coat, wellies and that. Ever handled a gun?'

'Not me,' said Mum.

'Not since I was in the cadet force at school,' said Dad. 'But I was a good shot then—champion target shooter two years running in fact.'

Caroline groaned. 'Dad! Don't start on that— please!'

'The girls aren't invited, I suppose?' said Mum.

'Afraid not. They're dangerous things, are guns. In fact, if you've never used one before, Mrs Ca . . .'

'Janet. Please!'

'If you've never used one, Janet, this time, if you don't mind me saying, you'll be best off just as a spectator.'

'I'm sure you're right. What will you be shooting?'

'Grouse it'll be.'

'Mmm!' Dad rubbed his belly enthusiastically. 'Makes a change from pheasant.'

'Aye.' Mr Metcalfe gave a sniff of a grin. 'Twenty-second October it is. Eleven o'clock sharp. Meet at the old Drovers Bridge. Packed lunch is all laid on, of course.'

Mum scribbled the details in big letters on her 'Country Diary' engagement calendar. 'Thank you so much, er . . .?'

'Bob,' said Mr Metcalfe curtly.

'Thank you so much, Bob! And please thank Sir Hugh. It really is kind.'

'Wants to keep his bank manager sweet, eh?' joked Dad.

'Aye well, there's many a true word spoke in jest.' Mr Metcalfe winked again at Sarah and then patted a cap neatly on top of his thick hair. 'Well, I'd best be on my road now. It's been nice to have a chat and that. Don't forget to pop round any time if there's anything we can ever do. Oh, and if you *could* keep a weather-eye open for any sign of these vandals . . .'

'We'll let you know at once,' promised Dad.

'That's good to know. Thanks for the coffe, er, Janet.'

He turned to go—just as someone gave a loud ring at the doorbell.

They all trooped into the hall and Mum opened the door. Ian was standing on the step.

'Well,' chuckled Mr Metcalfe, 'and here's *my* off-spring now! Ian, lad, yer daft ha'pporth, what are you doing here, eh? I'd have given you a lift, had I known you were coming.'

'It's all right, I ran,' said Ian. He didn't seem in the least bit put out, having to encounter the entire Carr family. 'Good practice for the athletics trials. Hi, Sarah.'

Sarah could feel Caz pinching her arm, painfully hard. 'Hello, Ian,' she said, as brightly as she could. She cleared her throat. 'Mum, Ian's in my class—can he come in?'

'No, no, *no!*' hissed Caz in her ear.

'Of course, love!' cried Mum. 'How lovely to have a friend nearby. Well, it's goodbye then, Bob—and thank you again—and welcome, Ian.'

Mr Metcalfe climbed into his muddy landrover and leaned out of the window. 'Be polite now, lad, don't disgrace yer dad!'

Ian poked his tongue out and was rewarded with a hearty slap across the shoulders. Sarah stared at them, envying their relationship.

'Well, Ian, would you like a cold drink or something?' offered Mum as the gamekeeper drove off and the Carrs all went back inside.

Caroline threw him an undisguised filthy look and walked pointedly out of the room.

Ian blinked after her. 'Er . . . no thanks, Mrs Carr.'

'Why don't we go out to the garden,' said Sarah quickly. 'There's quite a wild bit at the end. 'We get frogs in the pond. And sometimes we see squirrels.'

Ian followed her silently outside. They crossed the close cropped lawns, past neat, bright flowerbeds.

'Smarter than ours,' he remarked. 'Not a weed in sight.'

'It's Mum's hobby.'

'Oh. Aye.'

Aslan lorded his way across their path, stretching lazily in the sunshine.

'Ah, there's your cat,' said Ian. 'That won't encourage the squirrels. Is he a good mouser?'

'I'm not sure.' She didn't like to think about Aslan hunting down other creatures. 'He . . . he never brings anything indoors.'

'Not much point in having a cat if he can't keep the vermin down,' said Ian matter of factly.

'He's a pet, that's all! We just like his company. But I forgot—you don't like cats, do you?'

Ian grinned. 'It's all my dad's going on about them, I guess. Sorry!'

'But supposing—when you're a vet—people will bring you their sick cats.'

'Oh well, you've got to be professional when you're working with animals. You can't pick and choose which ones to treat.'

Good, thought Sarah, I'll throw that back at him soon. She'd got over her agitation now: she could feel her mind sharpening.

They came to the ornamental pond and sat down in the shade of an ancient, spreading apple tree.

'We private here?' asked Ian.

'Fairly.'

'What about your snooty sister?'

Sarah shrugged.

'OK then, you must have guessed what I've come about. Have you been watching for these animal rights nutters?' He pulled a small notepad and pencil out of his shirt pocket. 'Anything to report?'

Sarah watched him indignantly. Who did he think he was, taking notes on her?

'I have been watching,' she said uncomfortably. It was quite true, she had put up a charade once or twice of going out to spy when she saw people going through the gate, up to the hill. Pretending to herself as well as to Ian, she supposed. 'But not very much, I must admit. Every time I saw someone, it just turned out to be the shepherd—or that old couple with a sausage-dog who live in the village. Anyway, I just heard your dad asking my parents to keep a look out for the vandals—so I can't see the point of having our own secret investigation. Can't we leave it to him?'

'Dad's too wishy-washy about it,' said Ian. But by the way he said it, she guessed that the real reason for his spying was the simple desire to play detective. She relaxed a little: perhaps it was just a bit of a game to him, after all.

'Too fixed to his regular routine,' Ian went on. He looked at his watch. 'Like, I can tell you sure as sure, right now he'll be off up the hill checking all his traps.'

Sarah's heart missed at least two beats.

They'd be in for it! Mum, Dad, Mr Metcalfe—everyone knew that she and Caz had been on the hill just now. When he found the broken snare—surely he'd put two and two together! Unless . . . She kept her face set, but her mind spun, fast. She was already a double-agent, OK, she was already at risk. Well, perhaps she didn't have much left to lose; but there was her own skin to save (yes, and Caz's too) and—most importantly—a fox's life in the balance.

'In that case,' she said carefully, 'he'll find out for

himself what I was just about to tell you to tell him. Although I haven't actually seen anyone—I think they've been at it again.'

'What?'

'At the traps.'

'I never said you could go snooping round my dad's traps! He'll go spare!'

'No no, I haven't. I, um, don't even know where they are.' She winced at the lie, but she meant it for the best. 'You see, Caz and I have just been out walking and we found something. An injured fox.'

'So how do you . . . ?'

'Its leg was all cut and bleeding. It . . . it looked as if it might have been caught in a snare—and then cut free. They—someone—might have freed it and then just run away and left it.'

'You see!' cried Ian, 'that's typical of them ignorant animal rights folk—they haven't really got the animals' interests at heart at all. I mean, my dad goes round all the traps once or sometimes twice every day to check if anything's caught in them, and if there is, he'll finish them off, quick and clean, with a knock on the head, put them out of their misery. So what does this high and mighty liberation bunch do? Frees the thing, oh yeah, then just *leaves* it to die in *agony, slowly.*' He bit his lip with genuine bitterness. 'It could take two or three days until its suffering finishes, Sarah.'

'But it won't,' said Sarah.

'How do you know?'

'Because we rescued it, me and my sister.'

'*Rescued* it?'

'We carried it down from the hill on a sort of stretcher.'

'Huh? You kidding?'

'No!' Sarah rode on the crest of a wave, thrilling to their achievement and the cleverness of the story. 'We bundled it in our jackets and strapped it to a stretcher made of branches and things.'

'Blimey! Didn't it bite you?'

'It tried at first. But most of the time it was unconscious.'

'Well, if this is true . . .' Ian could scarcely hide his admiration. 'Where is it now?'

'Hidden in the bracken, by the gate opposite.'

'What you gonna do with it then?'

Sarah looked him straight in the eye. He believed her, he really believed her story!

'Hand him over to you, I hope,' she said. 'To your animal hospital.'

'Yeah,' said Ian, 'that would be something!' He grinned and shook his head. 'But what's my dad gonna say? A fox! He *hates* foxes! He'll never let me keep it.'

'You've got to be professional when you're working with animals,' Sarah reminded him. 'You can't pick and choose which ones to treat. You just said so yourself.'

Ian looked doubtful.

'Can't you convince him it's all vital experience for your future?'

'I could work on him, I suppose. But hey, Sarah, my dad was here just now: why ever didn't you tell him all this yourself?'

'I . . . I'm shy of him I suppose. And I couldn't possibly say anything like that in front of my mum and dad. They'd have fifty fits if they knew we'd been near a fox!'

Ian laughed. 'Molly-coddlers are they, wrapping their little girls up in cotton wool?'

'That's about it.'

'But what about your funny sister, eh? Perhaps she's not all bad if she was in on this with you.'

'Oh—she's mostly all right, is Caz.'

'Why's she always so stand-offish then—so downright rude?'

Sarah thought back to their argument on the way up to the hills. Why shouldn't she get her own back?

'Boy-friend trouble I expect.'

Ian guffawed and stood up. 'Well, I'd best be getting back now. Look, I can't promise anything, but try bringing it round after lunch and we'll see what my dad says.'

Chapter Nine

Sarah found her sister hunched on her bed, quaking with fury. Caroline shook back her curtain of hair and spat out her greeting like an angry cat.

'*Traitor!* Sarah, how could you? Of all people to be friends with—that . . . that *scab!*'

'I'm not a traitor,' said Sarah.

'Go away!'

'Don't talk like that to me. I've just saved us from being found out—and maybe saved the fox too.'

Caroline slid off the bed and stood to face her.

'You'd better explain what you mean.'

'Listen, Ian just told me his dad's gone up the hills—like *now*—to check the traps. Everyone knew we'd just been up there, didn't they? So when he finds the one we wrecked, he's bound to put two and two together. So I told him, before anyone could start wondering, that we found the fox—but I made out that it was after *someone else* had already freed him.'

Caroline swallowed. 'Did he believe you?'

'Yup,' said Sarah, 'he's got every reason to.'

'Why?'

'Because he thinks I'm on his side. See, why he's been getting so friendly with me—I've let him think that I'm helping him to catch the saboteurs!'

Caroline stared at her for a full minute. 'Phe-ee-ew,'

she said slowly. 'Perhaps—look, I'm sorry, I admit I've underestimated you, Sarah. That's clever.'

'Thanks.'

'But there's just one thing that bugs me about this revelation,' said Caroline. She sat down again and rubbed her chin thoughtfully. 'Who's side are you *really* on?'

'Oh, for goodness' sake!' cried Sarah, 'It's so stupid how you keep on asking me this. I'm on the *animals'* side, Caz, aren't you?'

Caroline sighed. 'Yes. Of course. I shouldn't keep . . . it's just that—well, we used to do everything together once, but you're getting so secretive and devious these days. And—oh hell, I guess I'm just generally upset.'

'About Mum and Dad going shooting?'

'Yes. It wouldn't be so bad if they were just neutral about the whole thing—but they're making every effort to get really involved. It's like a kick in the face for everything we believe in.'

'I suppose it hasn't even occurred to them that we wouldn't like it,' said Sarah. 'They're just so anxious to get in with all the local people.'

'Now you're sticking up for them!'

'Oh shut up!' said Sarah. 'Let's stick to talking about what really matters—Fox.'

'Right!'

'Listen then. You know I said I might have someone who could nurse it better? Well, you're not going to like this. It's Ian Metcalfe!'

Caroline opened her mouth, but Sarah went on in a rush before she could say anything.

'You know he keeps this sort of sanctuary for sick and injured wild animals in his yard? He wasn't that

87

keen on having a fox because his dad hates them so much, but he agreed in the end, and . . .'

'But this is . . .'

'Shut up, Caz! The poor animal's in agony right now; we haven't got time to argue on points of principle. If we want to save him, we'd better get organized into getting him to Ian's place because he's expecting us this afternoon.'

Caroline smoothed back her hair and sighed.

'OK. Let's get changed back into our jeans then— and get moving.'

The fox was still hidden in the dead bracken, more or less where they had left it; but it had changed position slightly and now its eyes were half open. It watched the girls, yellow with fear and suspicion. Its muscles were tense and it bared its teeth in an ugly snarl; but it was still panting helplessly.

'He looks dangerous,' said Sarah.

'Let's try coaxing him again. Don't let him think we're afraid. Make out we're in control of the situation.'

They inched forward.

'Here, boy, here, boy, it's all right.' Sarah held out her fingers encouragingly.'We should have brought him something to eat.'

'Hang on, I think I've got a few bits of biscuit in my pocket,' said Caroline.

'Do foxes eat biscuits?'

'Town foxes scavenge dustbins: they eat anything. Here, you can have the honour of offering them to him.'

Gingerly, Sarah took a biscuit and held it out. The fox still snarled, but now saliva dripped from its mouth. Suddenly it yanked forward, snatched the offering from her, and devoured it ravenously.

'Ow! I thought he was going to take my finger with it!'

'Well done,' said Caroline. 'You're braver than me. I've lost my nerve a bit since that stoat. Hey, but he must be thirsty too.'

'We could bring him water from the beck,' said Sarah.

'What in? We really need one of Aslan's bowls.'

They looked around.

There were quite a few odd fragments of rubbish scattered about: empty cans and packets, the sort of mess that careless daytrippers chucked over the wall without a thought for pollution. But just now, the girls were glad to see it.

'A yoghurt carton!' cried Sarah. She picked it up, clambered down to the stream and crouched on the slithery stones to fill it. She brought it back and offered it to the fox.

The animal's raging thirst got the better of its distrust. It lapped the water greedily, draining it dry in seconds.

'You'd best get more.'

While Sarah was filling it again, Caroline gave a sudden shriek.

'Caz! What is it? Has he bitten you?'

'No—but I thought he was going to get away then . . . only he can't really move after all, can't do any . . . His leg, it's so *horrible*. The wound's crawling with flies.' Her voice choked. 'Hurry up, Sarah: I don't think he can bear it much longer.'

At last the worst of the fox's thirst seemed satisfied.

'How can anyone *do* this to him Sarah?'

'Getting worked up won't help him,' said Sarah fiercely. 'Come on, we've got to do more awful things before he can be getting better—and he looks as if he still won't trust us an inch.'

They bundled up the fox in their jackets again; and then there was only one way to get it back onto the stretcher, and that was to push and shove it like a piece of meat. They did it at last, trying their best not to put any pressure on the bad leg. When the task was done, they could hear it making angry noises from inside the cover.

'Right,' said Sarah, taking charge again. 'The sooner we get to Ian's place, the better.'

Along the road, a couple of cars passed them, the drivers staring in amazement at their load; but luckily no one stopped to ask questions.

'This is his house,' said Sarah. She balanced the stretcher on one shoulder and unlatched the gate with her free hand, feeling the same apprehension as on her first visit. No, it was worse this time, much worse: she was really playing with fire now.

'Well, shall we put him down? I . . . I'll just ring the bell.'

They deposited the stretcher carefully on the gravel. In the kennels behind the house, the gundogs set up their usual barking.

'Look, if Ian's dad comes . . .' began Caroline; and at that very moment the door clicked open—to reveal Bob Metcalfe himself.

'Aye, and supposing he does!' he grinned at them. 'What am I, an ogre or . . .?' His eye fell on the stretcher with the twitching, grunting bundle strapped to it, and his expression changed to amazement.

'Blimmin' 'eck! What the hell's that supposed to be?'

'It's a fox,' said Sarah.

Mr Metcalfe caught his breath. 'Is it now? Well! The only good fox is one that's dead, in my book . . .'

'But when we were talking that time, you said . . .' protested Sarah.

'. . . and by the looks and sounds of something jumping about,' he went on, ignoring her, 'that one isn't. Am I right?'

'We rescued it,' said Sarah.

'Rescued it? A *fox* of all things?'

Sarah glanced at Caroline, but for once her older sister was leaving all the sweet talking to her. She thought she'd best grab the bull by the horns and say at once where they'd got it.

'Yes. We found it this morning, up the hills. With an injured leg. It looks . . .'

Bob Metcalfe marched out. With more gentleness than they would have expected, he pulled a corner of the covers off the animal and crouched to stare at it.

'I'll tell you what it looks like—like the one them vandals must have freed when they slashed my traps this morning!'

'Oh!' Sarah tried her best to look shocked: it wasn't too difficult, because she could feel herself turning hot and cold and hot again under the gamekeeper's scrutiny.

'Oh! Aye, that's what I thought when I found they'd been at their dirty tricks again. Well! And what have you two young lasses brought the thing here for?'

'We couldn't possibly have left him there,' said Caroline. She spoke slowly, emphasizing all the important words. 'In *agony*, Mr Metcalfe. Dying a slow, painful death. Imagine what it would be like for him.' She turned to let Sarah finish.

'Ian said—this morning, when I told him about it—that he could look after it in his animal hospital.'

'He did, did he?' The gamekeeper turned and yelled back into the darkness of his cottage. 'Ian! IAN! Here, lad, I want you—now!'

Ian appeared at the door, blinking at the girls.

'So you really brought it!' he said. 'Blimmin' 'eck!'

'Now what's all this about?' said his father. He sounded gruff, yet they could sense the good humour beneath it. 'The young ladies say you expect me to let you keep a live fox on our premises. Heh?'

'Just while it's sick,' said Sarah quickly. 'It'll be wonderful experience, Ian, for when you're a vet—won't it?'

'Hmph!' said Mr Metcalfe. 'It'll be some experience all right when it gets its teeth round Sir Hugh's best pheasants.'

'There's none of his birds in the yard, Dad,' said Ian reasonably. 'I've never nursed such a big animal before—it would be really interesting to take it on.'

'Hmph,' said Mr Metcalfe again. He looked doubtfully at the fox, and then studied the two girls. 'You deserve a bit of credit for initiative, mind,' he said grudgingly, 'and courage too. Seems a shame after all the effort you've gone to, and whatever you might think to the contrary, it pains me bad to see a mortal creature suffering. Question is, though, would it be better for the fox if I finished him off quick and cleanly now?'

'No!' cried Sarah. 'You've got to give him a chance to live—please, *please.*'

Mr Metcalfe gave her a soft, sad smile. He turned to Ian. 'What do you think, son? You're master of the hospital. Reckon you can really handle it? It'll be a vicious job, this one.'

Ian nodded. 'I'll wear my gauntlets. I'll take it really slow. I'm not scared.'

Mr Metcalfe considered the situation for a few more moments.

'All right then,' he said at last, 'you can take him, Ian. But mind this: any fox is an enemy of mine, and you're not spending a penny of our money feeding it, right? And if you nurse him better, you'd best think hard what you're going to do with him; for if I find him roaming my patch, pet or no pet, he'll end up in the snares again, or looking down the barrel of a gun. Understand?'

'Aye,' said Ian—with more sorrow than Sarah would have expected.

'All right, girls?'

Caroline, staring at the ground, shook her head so slightly that Mr Metcalfe didn't even notice. Sarah bit her lip. 'Yes,' she whispered.

'Right then. I'll leave you to get on with it.' He disappeared into the house.

'You'd best bring him round the back,' said Ian. He left them to carry the stretcher, leading the way past the kennels and through the gate, into the yard.

By the time they had staggered through, he already had a large cage ready with the door open. He pulled on a pair of thick leather gauntlets like a falconer wears.

'Right. Just put him down inside. I'll take over now.'

They slipped the stretcher gently into the cage.

Ian crawled in, loosened the bundle and pulled the covers off the fox. It lolled on the ground, its eyes glazed, its jaws snapping angrily, helplessly.

Ian muttered softly to it under his breath. He reached for a thick stick and pushed it into its half-open mouth as if he were giving a bone to a dog. The fox sank its teeth into it.

'Hey, Sarah—see that tap in the corner?'

'Yes.'

'There's some tin bowls by it. Fill us one with water. Bring it here. And there's a box of clean rags in that empty cage by the back door. It's open. Bring us a handful.'

She hesitated.

'*Quickly.*'

She got what he needed. Ian crouched over the fox, cleaning its bad leg. The shock of cold water on the wound seemed to make the animal swoon: its eyes closed and the stick fell from its jaws. Ian seized the opportunity to work more firmly.

'You seem to know what you're doing,' remarked Caroline; but she couldn't keep the resentment out of her voice.

Ian glanced up at her. 'It's a nasty one this. Reckon the rot's already set in—gangrene maybe.'

'*Please*, Ian,' said Sarah, 'do everything you can to try and save him.'

He gave an impatient grunt. 'Pity him or his mate didn't have as much sympathy as you when they went scrounging after eggs last spring. Scrunched up a dozen nests, they did—and managed to kill a couple of hen pheasants too, for the hell of it.'

He finished cleaning the wound, tore off some fresh

94

strips of rag, and used them to bind the stick to the fox's leg like a splint.

'Right, best be out of the way now.' He crawled backwards out of the cage. 'Fetch us a clean bowl of water for him to drink—and pour this one down that drain.'

Sarah ran about, doing everything he asked. He put the clean water inside, then snapped the cage door shut.

The fox lay inside, shivering, eyes half opening, drifting in and out of consciousness. Ian watched it critically.

'He'll take some nursing, he will—and some feeding up.' He gave Sarah a friendly slap across the shoulders and flashed a mirthless smile at Caroline. 'Seeing as you rescued him and brought him here, he's like your charge, OK? So how's about you take care of bringing him his food?'

'*Us?*' said Sarah.

'How do you feed the other animals you keep here?' asked Caroline.

'Well, they're mostly small things like birds and rabbits and bats, so they're no trouble: worms, corn, grass, flies'—he winked at Sarah—'that sort of thing. But foxes are different now. Meat eaters, they are.'

'Can't you give him tinned dog food?' suggested Sarah.

'Yeah, I *could*,' said Ian. He stared Caroline straight in the eye. 'But you heard what Dad said about feeding him: I can't really see him agreeing to share his best gundogs' dinner with Arch Enemy Number One—can you?'

'So—what then?' said Sarah.

'You'll have to bring things for him—like nice juicy rabbits.'

'Rabbits?' cried Sarah. 'You want *us* to catch rabbits?'

'Aye,' said Ian calmly.

'But we can't possibly! We couldn't go round killing animals. Not . . . not even for *him*. It's against everything we believe in. Isn't there something else he could have?'

Ian shook his head solemnly.

'Nope. It's fresh meat he needs. I mean—who ever heard of a vegetarian fox?'

Chapter Ten

The look on Ian's normally gentle face was threatening. It made Sarah feel nervous. She wasn't surprised when he suddenly burst out.

'Blimmin' 'eck, what the hell do you know about animals?—yeah, you too Sarah! Do you honestly think things out in the wild live all cosily side by side, like in one of them soppy stories for tiny kids? I mean, the different sorts, they spend most of their time killing each other. They've got to kill to eat, to stay alive themselves. That's what foxes are, *meat eaters*. Just like people—like you and me.'

'We don't eat meat,' said Sarah loftily.

Ian shrugged. 'Well, that's your loss. Anyway, come away from the yard. I reckon that fox needs some peace and quiet if he's to stand any chance of getting better.'

He led them out, back through the iron gate.

'You're very clever on the nursing side, Ian,' said Caroline suddenly, 'but you've got no business to make out that you know more than we do about animals. My sister and I have studied wildlife for a long time, you know.'

Ian's face twitched as if he couldn't decide whether to laugh or have another outburst.

'O-ooh,' he said at last, speaking all high pitched

like a girl, 'we have studied a lot of things then, haven't we!' His voice sank to its normal tone again. 'Look, Caz or Snaz or whatever you call yourself, I don't know what I've ever done to get your back up, but I'm fair fed up with the hoity-toity way you always speak to me. Right? If you want me to look after this fox of yours, you'd better cut it out. *Right?*'

Caroline coloured and opened her mouth.

'OK, OK,' said Sarah quickly. 'Please, Ian—Caz—don't make an argument. What's the point?'

They were at the main gate that led from the drive to the road. Ian's face was set. He unlatched it without another word and began to usher them out.

Suddenly his arm shot out and he had them both pinned back against the gate, like that time in the wood with the badgers.

'What do you think you're—?' yelled Caroline indignantly.

At once Ian's other hand was clapped over her mouth.

'Sshh! Shut up! Use your eyes—*there*!'

'What?' whispered Sarah. Then: 'Oh, Caz, yes—look!'

A stoat had darted out from the hedge. Now it waited, stopped dead in the middle of the road. It lifted its head and sniffed the air.

A rabbit bounded out from the opposite hedge, perhaps fifty metres away, oblivious to danger.

In a flash, the stoat was after it. The rabbit saw the movement—hesitated—ran. They zig-zagged madly across the road and back again, the stoat gaining steadily on its prey. The rabbit stopped. For a moment, the stoat stopped too. They could see its small dark eye gleaming. Then it moved forward again. Now the rabbit was frozen, its eye transfixed as if held by some evil, invisible power. It screamed, with an anguish that was enough to curdle the blood.

Then the stoat pounced and the scream stopped.

Ian let out his breath. 'Bites it in the back of the neck,' he whispered. 'Nice clean death. Just one blow. Don't often get the chance to see it—you're lucky! Not bad, heh?'

'It was foul,' said Caroline sharply.

'But that's nature!' said Ian. He made no effort to disguise the contempt in his voice or his face. 'You just told me you're the great wildlife experts. You can't pick and choose which animals you fancy, if you really care about them, heh?'

'Caz,' said Sarah, 'you've got to agree that that stoat needs its food as much as the rabbit does . . . er, did. Like poor Fox.'

'Your father takes it upon himself to pick and choose which animals should live and die though,' said Caroline icily.

Ian turned on her. 'Right on! It's a pity that animal liberation bunch can't stop and watch something like that—*then* they'd see why he traps things like stoats and foxes and rats and weasels! What it did to that rabbit, it'll do to the grouse and pheasant chicks too, see? "Kill a stoat, give a rabbit a chance to live"— how about that for a slogan?'

'Look,' cried Sarah, 'it's dragging the rabbit across the road! How can it manage? It looks so heavy: the rabbit's much bigger than the stoat.'

'Aye, it's strong as it's clever,' said Ian. 'Clever like us.' He slipped back through the gate. 'Well, I'll be seeing you again soon then. You know what to do— what you've got to bring round, like, if you want that old fox to live, heh? If you can't make it, Dad and I will just have to put him out of his misery. Might be the best thing, actually—end his suffering quickly and kindly.' He faced them squarely, hands thrust in his pockets. 'That's all experience for me too. Got to learn not to cry when you're a vet—eh, Sarah?'

He turned and sprinted back up to his cottage.

The girls set off for home, walking in silence.

'Well?' said Sarah at last.

'Well!' said Caroline. 'I always guessed he was a creep! So callous . . .'

'What's that?'

'Uncaring. Quite happy to bump the poor thing off. Typical gamekeeper attitude.'

'But you must admit he's clever,' said Sarah, 'and he knows a lot. I mean, *we* wouldn't have the first idea how to nurse bats and birds and things, let alone foxes.'

'We handled Fox all right,' said Caroline defensively. 'We got him there safely.'

'It was pretty haphazard though. We couldn't look after him ourselves, not at home.'

Caroline laughed. 'Can you imagine? Mum and Dad would go bananas! It was hard enough persuading them to let us have Aslan, let alone *wild* animals. That Ian's got it all made for him there. At least his dad's not bothered about animals, even if he does go round slaughtering them.'

'He seems to get on really well with his dad,' said Sarah wistfully.

'Too well if you ask me,' said Caroline. 'We can't trust him, Sarah—not even to look after poor old Fox.'

'But you must admit,' said Sarah, 'that so long as I

make out I'm friends with him, he's less likely to suspect what we're up to.'

'Hmph.'

They walked on.

'Anyway,' said Sarah after a few minutes, 'about this food for Fox. We must do something.'

'Why don't we just buy some tins of dog food?' said Caroline. 'Surely he'd eat that.'

'I bet Ian would refuse to give it to him on principle,' said Sarah. 'Anyway, all dog food has meat in it, doesn't it? What's the difference?'

'At least we wouldn't have killed it with our own hands.'

'Coward! So you're happy to pay for someone else to kill it? We might as well go back to eating meat ourselves in that case.'

'OK, OK,' sighed Caroline, 'let's think again. Oh— I know—car accidents!'

'Huh?'

'You know, the road's always littered with poor dead rabbits knocked down by cars. Surely Fox could eat some of those.'

Sarah thought. 'Ye-es. You mean—if they're dead already, we're not doing anything wrong in using them as food?'

'They're carrion,' said Caroline. 'We're doing the countryside a favour, clearing them up.'

'You're right. Yes, let's do that, Caz—if we can find any, that is.'

'We'll go back, get our bikes out, and go looking.'

They spent the next hour cycling up and down the lanes around their house. Caroline was right: the road *was* littered with road casualties; but most of them had been killed so long ago they were merely squashed heaps of fur and bones, the flesh long finished off by crows and flies.

In the end, however, they managed to find two rabbits and a hedgehog that looked fairly fresh and whole. They scooped them carefully into plastic bags, then dumped the lot into Caroline's saddle-bag.

'We'd best take them straight to Ian's,' said Caroline, 'before Mum and Dad start poking their noses in.'

'All right. But I don't want to talk to him again—or his dad!'

'Then we'll leave them on the doorstep—but we'd better write a note.'

Sarah giggled. 'Yes! Otherwise, if his dad found it, he might think it was an insulting gift from the animal liberationists—you know, like louts who go posting muck through their enemies' letterboxes.'

Caroline raised her eyebrows, 'We won't be stooping to that level, thank you!'

'Oh, don't be so high-and-mighty serious! Here, let's have some paper, if you've got any.'

Caroline pulled a pencil and a squashed school exercise book out of her saddle-bag. 'Tear a sheet from that.'

Sarah scribbled quickly, then waved it at her.

> *Dear Ian, Here is some food for the fox.*
> *Yours sincerely, Sarah and Caz.*

'OK?'

'OK.'

They rode back furiously to the Gamekeeper's Cottage. Caroline leaped off her bike, dumped the plastic bags on the doorstep with the note carefully wedged on top—and then they were wheeling off again, almost before the dogs could start barking.

There was fish for supper. 'I hope that's all right for you?' said Mum politely (rather *too* politely, Sarah thought: was she being patronizing again?); 'Only you haven't actually told me yet whether fish is, um, acceptable for you.'

What with everything else, they hadn't had a chance to talk about it yet. A picture flashed into Sarah's mind of a fish dangling and struggling helplessly from an angler's hook. She looked to Caz for support.

'We'll eat it,' said Caroline quickly.

So that was that. Sarah sat over her meal, trying to enjoy it. She remembered seeing a couple of fishing rods propped up in a corner of Ian's hall. *He* had no qualms about eating meat, or anything; yet ironically he was probably doing more to help wild animls than they were.

Dad abruptly broke into her thoughts. He was in one of his expansive, happy moods, full of the joys of country living.

'Bought myself some breeches today, and green wellies,' he said. 'All ready for the big shoot! And one of those dirty brown thorn-proof jackets that everyone seems to have.'

Mum groaned. 'Oh John, you'll turn into one of these Green Wellie Brigade types!' She looked to the girls to share the teasing of him, but neither of them responded.

'No, honestly,' said Dad, 'everyone wears them round here. There's nothing pretentious about them. Even the gamekeeper chappie, old Bob Metcalfe's got

103

one. Practical they are, see. Keep the weather out—and big, roomy pockets.'

Sarah and Caroline ate steadily, ignoring the conversation.

'Oh come on, girls!' said Dad. He looked hurt. 'You're as dead as two doornails today. What's up with you, eh? Can't go round being gloomy in the countryside. This is one of England's loveliest corners, did you know that?'

They glanced at each other, and managed to force smiles at him.

'Anyway, talking of Bob Metcalfe,' Dad went on, 'he was telling me, Sarah, that his lad—Ian is it—wants to be a vet like you. Said he's got some animal sanctuary thing in his yard, and you're welcome to go round and help out any time. That's nice of him, isn't it?'

From the corner of her eye, Sarah saw Caz mouthing the word *traitor* at her. She stared at her mashed potato.

'I . . . I don't want to be a vet any more,' she said huskily.

'Why ever not?' cried Mum. 'You've been dead set on it up to now.'

Sarah felt tears welling up. Her mind was a whirlwind. She scraped back her chair and stood up, her voice breaking into a sob.

'Because they spend half their time putting innocent animals to sleep, that's why!'

Then she rushed out of the room and slammed the door shut behind her.

Chapter Eleven

At school Sarah and Ian had slipped into an unspoken agreement not to talk much to each other. But at Monday lunch time, as she was hurrying across the playground to join Karen and some of the other girls, he waylaid her.

'Hey, Sarah. I'd better tell you right now: Fox died.'

Her heart jolted. 'No! Ian—tell me it's not—that you're teasing?'

He shook his head. 'Why should I tease about that sort of thing? Death isn't funny.'

'What . . . what happened?'

'Starvation partly.'

'But how could he starve?' cried Sarah. 'We brought you things for him. We left them on the doorstep. Surely—you must have found them!'

Ian guffawed. 'How the hell do you expect a sick fox to cope with a hedgehog, eh? It's all prickles. What a daft thing to bring round!'

'But we brought you rabbits too.'

'Aye, and both of them mixy.'

'Pardon?'

'Oh come on now,' said Ian, looking genuinely shocked, 'surely you've lived out in the country long enough to know a mixy rabbit when you see one? Diseased, girl. Got the myxomatosis.'

'But the rabbits we got were run over! They didn't die of disease—we picked them up off the road.'

'Aye,' said Ian wearily, 'but couldn't you see they were sick before they got mown down? How couldn't you notice that their eyes were all puffed and swollen—that's the classic sign of mixy? You can't give a sick animal diseased meat to eat.'

Sarah blinked back the tears. 'Look, Ian, we didn't realize. All right, I'll admit we don't know much compared to you, but you must see that we did our best. Couldn't you have found something else to feed him on?'

Ian's face softened. 'Aye, of course we fed it,' he said. 'I'm not that heartless. Nor's my dad. But fact is, gangrene set in his bad leg. In the end there was no hope for him. We had to finish him off. Hey, don't cry, Sarah—it was quick, I swear it! He didn't know . . . I treated him kind, like.'

'You *beast*!' said Sarah. 'How can killing be *kind*?'

They said nothing more to each other for the next few days. But on Thursday Ian was the centre of attention once again.

'My old man's had the police out again: got a big search on. His blood's really up! These animal liberation nutters, they've been at it full force. Every night. Slashing up all the snares and traps. Stupid it is, real pointless. I mean, Dad's got piles of them stacked up in his shed—so every time one goes, he's straight out putting new ones in their place. Anyway, if they're nabbed, he's gonna stand right up in court, see they get the toughest punishment that's going!'

The whole class was jostling round him in the playground, some heckling, some cheering him on, just like last time. Through the sea of faces, his eyes met Sarah's for a moment.

'Hey look!' someone shouted suddenly, 'and here they are—police!'

They all whirled round as a white police car swung into the playground.

Ian screwed up his eyes against the sun, staring at the driver. 'It's the same one as came to see my dad.'

'Come to arrest Howard and his Animal Lib mates,' said Karen, 'for their dangerous views . . .' she cackled and made a Dracula-style grab at him '. . . and their bloodied hands. Heh, heh, heh!'

'Ho ho! Howard grimaced back at her; but everyone else was suddenly looking serious.

'Surely he's not looking for suspects here?' exlaimed Cathy.

Sarah tried to shrink back into the crowd.

'Why not?' said Karen. 'I mean, there's plenty who might be guilty.' She began to reel off a list of names: each one was greeted with melodramatic guffaws and general clowning around.

As discretely as she could, her mind jittering, Sarah drifted off towards the toilets before anyone could start to cross-examine her again.

Later, the policeman was glimpsed strolling down the corridor with the deputy head; then his unfamiliar voice was heard dimly first from this classroom, then from that. At last he came in to Sarah's class, and Miss Crewe introduced him.

'This is Sergeant Bainbridge. He's come to talk to you—to warn you, I think—about some, um, nasty goings-on roundabouts.'

The sergeant seated himself on Miss Crewe's desk and tried unsuccessfully to look like a cosy uncle. He nodded briefly at Ian and flashed him a mirthless smile.

'Aye, hello there. Well, I see young Metcalfe is in this class, so no doubt he's already given some or all of you an inkling of what this is going to be about. But in case he hasn't, I'll tell you straight. There's some nasty characters, hanging about up the dale. Causing damage to the estates, they are, sabotaging the game-keeper's property. They're fanatics, most likely—the sort that'll let nothing stop them from carrying out their misdeeds.'

Sarah sat listening to him, mesmerized.

'Now,' the policeman went on, 'I know a lot of you live right out on the farms and so on, in the outlying villages, and some, no doubt, in quite isolated spots. And it's my guess you maybe like to go roaming about on the hills. Well, my warning to you is this: *don't*—leastaways, not until we've caught this bunch of madmen. Going on past experience in other areas, they're likely to be pretty ruthless—and they'll give short shrift to anyone who they reckon might have seen them at their dirty work.'

He sniffed. 'Right, is my meaning clear? One: don't go wandering about the countryside on your own. Two: if you see anyone—anything—suspicious, keep well clear and get your mum or dad to phone us right away.'

Sarah felt light-headed, unreal. This wasn't them, it couldn't be! They'd hardly done anything—not on this scale: he was making them out to be barbarians! But supposing . . . supposing there were *other* people now, muscling in on the act, professional wreckers, who'd heard what they'd started and moved in? If they were linked with them, she and Caz could be in *real* trouble . . .

108

Chapter Twelve

Caroline's bedroom door was locked. Sarah knocked, then waited.

'Just a minute: who is it?'

'Only me.'

'Oh—Sarah! *You* can come in. Hang on, I'll unlock it.'

The key clicked and Sarah went in.

'Why are the curtains drawn? It's not dark yet.'

'I don't want ... Just in case anyone should walk past and see in,' said Caroline. Her voice had a broken edge to it. She tried to laugh, but it was dry and humourless.

Sarah blinked at her through the gloom, puzzled. Then her eye was caught by a neat arrangement of gleaming metal on the bed.

Caroline had laid out her set of tools. There were three pairs of wirecutters of different designs and sizes, a very small hack-saw, a pair of thick workman's gauntlets, a map and a small first-aid kit.

Sarah let her gaze wander over them. Their cold efficiency was incongruously softened by the way they lay cushioned on the pink duvet. She felt sick and nervous.

'But there's others doing our job now,' she said at last. 'That policeman at school today—you must have had the same talk as we did? Ian was telling everyone at lunchtime: they've been out every night this week. Our, um, campaign must have got famous, given other people the idea.' She stared at the wire cutters. 'Perhaps it's the *real* animal liberation people this time.'

'*We're* the real thing,' Caroline said fiercely.

'Oh, Caz, you know what I mean. Grown-ups. Militants. What does Dad call them—anarchists?'

'There's no one else,' said Caroline.

'But you've heard—they've been going out regularly apparently, doing loads of damage. If we got mixed up with them, Caz, we could be in real trouble!'

Caroline sat down next to the soft drapes and the shiny metal. Her legs and her voice were shaking.

'It was me,' she said.

'You?' Sarah felt her mouth drop open foolishly.'But you haven't been out at all this week!'

'I have. When you—and everyone—were asleep.'

'*When?*'

'Every night.'

'I don't believe it! What time?'

'Different times each night. Yesterday I set my alarm for two a.m.'

'I never heard you!'

'Nor did Mum and Dad, thank goodness.'

'Caz—if this is true—why haven't you told me?'

'I'm telling you now.'

'But you never asked me to come with you!'

'I didn't think you'd come. And I didn't want to risk getting you into trouble. Anyway, I haven't really felt I could trust you. You're Ian Metcalfe's friend.'

There was a long silence. Sarah felt scared now, really scared. She hadn't realized quite how desperate

110

Caz was to change things for the animals.

'You're going to get caught,' she whispered.

'I'm careful.'

'But the police are after you, Caz. It must be only a matter of time before they find you!'

'Like I said, I change the times each night. I cover my tracks. No one's going to suspect the bank manager's daughter!'

She got up and scooped the tools into a box. Her movements were unusually clumsy. She shoved the box under the bed, right to the back, and wedged an old pair of boots in front, to hide it.

'Are you going out tonight?' asked Sarah.

'I'm not saying.'

'Don't keep any more secrets from me, Caz!'

'*You* do. You're a double-agent. You said so yourself.'

'Please, Caz.'

'You can open the curtains now,' Caz said.

Sarah did so. A wonderful red sunset glowed into the room. Birds twittered peacefully in the bushes. And Sarah's stomach catapulted.

'Caz! There's a police car!'

'Where?'

'Parked opposite—by the footpath gate.'

'Oh gawd!'

'Don't go out tonight Caz—*please*.'

Caroline peered through the window beside her. Sarah could feel the tension in her whole body.

'All right. I . . . I'd better leave it tonight,' she said.

'You're not to go out any night this week,' urged Sarah. 'Not for a long time. *Promise* me, Caz.'

Caroline's face was very pale. She stood absolutely

still. Tears squeezed themselves out of her eyes and rolled silently down her cheeks.

'But the animals,' she said. 'Sarah, there must be others up there like poor Fox: think of them waiting, think of their pain. There's only us to save them. If we give up now . . .' Her voice tailed off while she cleared her throat. 'Last week, before I got started, every night I was lying awake imagining them. What I'm, what *we're* doing: it's not very much, just a tiny scratch at the surface—but we're their only hope.'

'But Caz, if we get arrested and . . . sent away, then we won't be able to help them at all. *Please* be sensible. Please leave off, just for a while.'

Caroline pulled a tissue out from her sleeve and dabbed at her eyes. 'OK. Perhaps in the long run you're right—I ought to lie low for a while.' She sighed. 'Look, I promise I'll leave it completely for a week or two, then maybe I'll go out at a different time—at the weekend. In daylight.' She flashed a sad smile at Sarah. 'You could even come with me—if you wanted to, that is.'

Sarah hesitated. The sick feeling came back.

'I . . . I don't think I do want to, Caz. I'm not sure whether I agree with it any more. I'm not sure whether messing around with the gamekeeper's work really is the best thing for the animals. I mean, Mr Metcalfe seems to understand the country much more than we do. I'm sure he's not deliberately cruel or anything.'

'You're entitled to your views, of course,' said Caroline. But she made no attempt to hide the disappointment in her voice.

'But . . . do you want me to help you?'

'Of course I want you to!' Caroline burst out. 'Every night, I've longed to have you with me! Can't you imagine how scary it is, trudging all the way up there in the dark, fiddling around with the traps, all on my own? And lonely! Heck, Sarah, just knowing you were there, even if you just stood watching—it would make all the difference!'

Sarah swallowed. Yes, she could imagine it all right: like a bad dream! Caz must be really brave, really dedicated—she deserved help, didn't she, not doubts and deceit, Sarah thought, which is what my main contribution seems to be. With a great effort, she swallowed and succeeded in pushing the sickness away.

'All right then,' she said, 'next time, I'll come.'

Chapter Thirteen

It was raining, pelting down. Mum thought they were loonies to be off walking on a day like this; but Caroline explained that it was a good opportunity to watch how wildlife reacted to the wet. Her class was doing a project on droughts and monsoons and things, she said (this was actually quite true) and she'd got really interested in it all.

Anyway, they managed to get off without any more questions; but Mum insisted they wore their full set of waterproof cagoules and over-trousers. This was a bit of a problem, since Caroline's were fluorescent orange, and Sarah's were an equally bright blue. They'd be seen miles away, moving about on the hills.

'We'll get up to the top of the footpath and then we'll take them off under the trees,' said Caroline.

'But we'll get soaked!' protested Sarah.

'Never mind, we'll take a change of dry clothing in the back-packs. We can hide the lot somewhere— waterproofs and all—and change on the way down.

There was another problem too.

On their way up, they met Bob Metcalfe.

'Hello, Sarah, Caroline!' He beamed at them with such friendliness that Sarah wanted to cry. 'Rough weather for a walk, isn't it?'

'I'm doing research for a school project,' Caroline

explained patiently. 'About how nature reacts to monsoons.'

The gamekeeper chuckled. 'Aye well, you could call this a monsoon, right enough! Watch where you're walking now girls—the path's slippery up top.' His face turned suddenly serious. 'And watch out, just in case, for any nasty characters hanging about. Vandals. You know the lot I mean.'

Sarah swallowed. 'You mean—the people who've been messing around with your traps?'

'That's the ones.'

'Are they still doing it?' asked Caroline innocently.

'Not for a week or two now. But they'll be back after a break, I'll be bound. No doubt it's the calm before the storm.' Suddenly he lifted the stick he was carrying and swung it with unexpected force against the wet earth. His voice deepened. 'Aye, and there'll be a fair old storm, I'm telling you, when I finally lay my hands on them. Scum they are, ignorant scum!'

'We'll be careful,' Sarah told him huskily. 'And, um, we'll let you know if we see anything suspicious.'

'That's good. But if you *do* see anyone—don't go approaching them now. They're dangerous maniacs, these types.'

He waved them off and hurried on his way.

Sarah and Caroline continued their slow climb up the hill. Rain streamed down their faces, seeped through the seams of their cagoules.

'We can't do it,' said Sarah at last, 'not now we've seen him!'

'He'll never suspect it's us.'

'He's bound to wonder . . . first he meets us going up the hill, and then his traps are damaged.'

They crossed the beck and came to the gate. Caroline climbed over it.

'Then we'll stop him before he even has a chance to wonder,' she said. 'As soon as we get back, you can ring Ian. Tell him you've seen signs of the vandals, as they call us—clues, you could say. Then you'll really be in his good books.'

'What signs? What clues? I can't . . . It would have to be convincing, something they can't disprove.'

'Oh, I don't know. Let's get on with what we've come for. We'll think of something on the way back.'

They stood facing each other over the gate.

'Look,' said Caroline, 'you promised to help me. Now you're trying to chicken out.'

'But . . . all I seem to be doing is more and more lying!'

'It won't be a lie,' said Caroline. 'We've seen the signs that we've made ourselves.'

'Don't be so sick—joking about it!'

'I'm not joking, Sarah. This is desperate. There's animals being killed by that Metcalfe man every day. On our doorstep. We've *got* to stop it. What else can we do?'

An image of the stoat pouncing swam into Sarah's mind.

'But the animals are killing each other too,' she whispered. 'They're no better than us.'

'Oh for goodness' sake, stop being sentimental! That's nature. That's how things are meant to be. Not this . . . this meaningless slaughter!'

She turned her back on Sarah, marched into the trees and pulled off her waterproofs angrily, stuffing them into the backpack. She moved quickly, efficiently, gracefully. There was a hollow tree root nearby, filled with a drift of leaves and pine needles. She scooped them out with her hands, like a rabbit burrowing, stuffed the bag into the hollow, then scattered the debris on top again.

'Desert me then! I don't care. See, I was right to come up on my own all those other times—I knew you didn't really want to.'

'I'm sure we'll be caught.' Sarah still hesitated. It was madness, madness, madness.

'I won't hold it against you if you don't come,' said Caroline loftily. 'Just hurry up and make up your mind, that's all.'

Sarah sighed. The wind sighed in the trees. She was scared—dead scared—but she would feel even worse about it, she thought, if she left Caz on her own, and then Caz got caught.

'Oh . . . All right then.'

She climbed over the gate, then pulled off her waterproofs and hid them, as Caroline had done.

'You could tell Ian you saw some bags and things like this hidden along the path,' said Caroline. 'That would be perfectly true.'

'Yes. All right.' Her mouth was dry as bones. Her conscience was numb.

They walked into the trees—briskly, because Caroline had been up here so many times now, she knew the way perfectly.

'I shouldn't think there'll be any animals in them this time,' Caroline said lightly, 'not if old Metcalfe's just been up here. He pulls out the ones he's trapped and strangles them, doesn't he, or smashes their skulls in, if they're not already dead.'

Sarah drew her breath in. 'I don't know.'

'I bet he loves doing it. I expect it gives him a kinky sort of pleasure, to make things die.'

'Caz, don't! Mr Metcalfe's not *like* that! He puts them to sleep painlessly.'

Caroline snorted.

Sarah followed her lifelessly. A great misery hung over her. She felt like a prisoner of war, condemned to fulfil some evil task under pain of death.

They moved and worked quickly. As Caroline had predicted, all the traps were empty, so it was simply a question of slicing through each one with the wire cutters, which took only a minute or two for each.

Caroline muttered a tally as they worked: 'Eight, nine . . . thirteen . . . That'll give him something to think about!'

They had come quite a long way—to the far edge of the wood, where a low dry-stone wall divided the trees from a rough pasture, sloping down to the next valley, grazed by black-faced sheep.

Sarah's misery was mounting. She felt all shivery with being soaked through, and as the tree cover thinned, increasingly jumpy and exposed to watching eyes.

'We'll just do this one, then we'll have a break,' Caroline said cheerfully. She looked flushed and exhilarated. I've got some of that new chocolate bar with nuts and coconut that you like.'

They bent over the snare together and snipped in unison.

As they straightened up, twigs crackled softly behind them.

'Well, well, well,' a woman's voice said, a rich, plummy voice they didn't recognize. 'And we all thought it was a gang of fifteen-stone heavies!'

118

Their eyes met. Caroline reached out to squeeze Sarah's hand, but Sarah pushed her angrily away. They turned round.

A middle-aged woman was watching them through narrowed eyes. She was tall and slim, her dark brown hair thickly streaked with grey, carelessly dressed in cord jeans, a man's hooded oilskin riding jacket and filthy green wellingtons. A smile played wryly about her lips, oozing an air of calm, no-nonsense confidence.

'Who are you?' Sarah blurted out stupidly—though she had already guessed with a dreadful sinking feeling.

'Me? I'm Frances Harryman.' Still the detached half-smile, but otherwise her face was a blank, and her pale eyes didn't waver from their faces. 'But more to the point: who are *you?*'

Sarah just stared at her; through a frozen blur of panic, she felt Caroline's hand on her arm, heard the yelled command: *'Run!'*

Then somehow they were both moving, dodging undergrowth and low branches until they reached the main broad track. Sarah could see Caz racing ahead; allowed herself a brief second to catch breath; then plunged forward with a super-human burst of speed.

Feet pounding, heart pounding, she heard a piercing whistle; then from somewhere behind, the woman calling, 'Hoy, hoy, hoy!' like a shout to the dogs that she'd often heard the hill shepherds use.

Running blindly, she collided suddenly into Caroline's back—'Caz! Don't stop!'—and a turmoil of barking.

Three sheepdogs surrounded them, crouching, inching forward, nosing them, leaping up threateningly when the girls tried to dodge.

119

Their way was barred forwards, sideways . . .

'We'll have to go back!' shouted Caroline; but even as they turned, Lady Frances Harryman came striding towards them through the rain.

'Come with me please!'

She grabbed Caroline's wrist with an impatient gesture and started to half drag her along. Caroline struggled to free herself, but Frances Harryman was unexpectedly strong. She gave an angry laugh: 'That'll *do!*' as if Caroline were no more than an animal she was breaking in. The dogs got up and trotted behind, leaving Sarah staring after the strange group in disbelief.

One caught, both found guilty—surely? Anyway, she couldn't desert Caz now . . .

Meekly, like a lamb walking into the slaughter-house, she followed.

Chapter Fourteen

The Harryman's house loomed ahead. It was a big old hunting lodge, all grey stone and enormous windows, set in carefully landscaped gardens.

Lady Harryman marched them towards a side door. It swung open easily at a touch, but she locked it quickly behind them and pocketed the key. They were in a broad, carpeted passage that smelt luxuriously of polish.

She stopped briefly to remove boots and jacket and to rub the dogs down with grubby towels; then she ushered the girls smartly through a door at the far end.

It led into a study with two big bay windows overlooking the hills, and three walls lined with files and books. In one window stood a rather battered antique desk, submerged under a scatter of papers; in the other there was a leather sofa and two armchairs.

'Well then.' Lady Harryman compressed her lips tightly. 'We may as well sit down.'

She pointed to the sofa and waited, arms akimbo, while Sarah and Caroline seated themselves, then lowered herself into one of the chairs opposite. The three collies slumped quietly under the desk.

For an age she just stared at them thoughtfully while the rain drummed drearily on the windows.

Sarah looked at the floor, desperately trying not to fidget because it made the leather sofa creak.

'So,' said Lady Harryman at last, 'what are your names?'

Sarah opened her mouth to answer, hesitated, saw Caz shaking her head urgently, and shut it again.

Lady Harryman sniffed. 'You reckon there's safety in silence, eh? Where's all the great bravado gone? Have you really got nothing to say for yourselves? Nothing to justify your pathetic little pranks?' She leaned back lazily and placed her fingertips together. 'What are you then—just common vandals, breaking up other people's property to keep yourselves from being bored? I hope you feel thoroughly ashamed of yourselves.'

Sarah's throat burned dry and dumb with humiliation. She looked helplessly at her sister.

Caroline was licking her lips. A flush spread slowly across her face.

'Ashamed?' she said huskily, 'we've got nothing to be ashamed of! It's *you*—you and your husband and your horrible gamekeeper and all the other people who find it fun to go around killing things—murdering innocent animals!'

Lady Harryman laughed out loud.

'Don't you laugh at us!' Caroline sounded tense and breathless. 'I suppose you're going to call the police in a minute, get us arrested? Well, I can tell you this: I'm not scared to go to prison for what I beieve in! But just hear me out before you get rid of us like all your other so-called vermin—right?'

'Go on then. I'm not in a hurry.'

The laugh dissolved into an expression of unexpected pleasantness and for a moment Caroline was thrown. She swallowed.

'We've done what we did because we love animals. We can't bear what you do to them—not just shooting the birds, though that's bad enough, but what your gamekeeper does with his traps. We've seen it—with our own eyes.

'We rescued a fox that was caught in one of the snares. It was in a dreadful state!' She turned her face suddenly, and Sarah saw that her eyes were bright with tears. 'How would you like to spend hours with a piece of wire boring into your leg until it's half cut off, and then the flies start crawling round it, and nothing to eat or drink, and then die of gangrene the next day? That's what happened to our fox.'

Lady Harryman looked back at her seriously.

'Wretched, isn't it? I know Bob Metcalfe does his utmost to keep suffering to the minimum, but . . .'

'Then you agree with us!' cried Caroline. 'So how can you let . . .'

'Of course I agree with your repulsion against unnecessary suffering! Look, woman to woman as it were, isn't it against all our instincts to hurt any creature? But the trouble is, in real life, black and white arguments just don't work: there are always choices to be made, the lesser of two evils . . .'

'There's nothing more evil than torturing an animal to death!'

'No?' said Lady Harryman. 'Well, that's a matter of opinion. I happen to think that the most evil thing in the world at the moment is the way the countryside— the whole environment—is being destroyed. You seem to be pretty passionate about what I suppose you would call animal rights; well, what *I* believe in covers

123

that plus a whole lot more too: I'm a passionate conservationist. So is my husband. That's why we use our estate mainly for raising birds for the shoot.'

'That's mad! It's mad, wicked lies!' Caroline spluttered through her outrage. 'Conservation isn't about shooting and trapping. It's about letting things live!'

Lady Harryman laughed again. 'Exactly. Look, Hugh and I own all this land. We want to keep it natural, unspoiled, how it's always been; but somehow we've got to make it pay as well. It's damned expensive running a big estate, and even though you probably think we're stinking rich, even for us, money doesn't grow on trees. So we let out the shooting rights, sell off some of the surplus birds we raise. That way we can justify—in terms of earning a living I mean—justify keeping the land wild, full of trees and hedges and wetland, even patches of untouched moors, because that's just what grouse and pheasants need. What wild creatures like songbirds and mice and voles as well as your beloved foxes need too. At least they have a chance to roam free, live a natural, decent life—even if (I'm sorry about this, believe me) some of them do end up in Bob's traps because otherwise they'd do too much damage to the shoot.'

'But that's rubbish!' cried Caroline. 'You could use the land just for ordinary farming—farms have hedges. Or why can't you just plant it all over with tress and sell the wood?'

'Farming?' said Lady Harryman. 'Well, my dear, most farmers these days seem to be ripping out all their trees and hedges and spraying all the wild plants to death: they say it's the only way to make the land efficient enough to pay its way. And as for growing wood, to make any money you need to plant nasty thick forests of those quick growing pines; and I can assure you there's not many animals or birds—hardly any flowers even—can survive under their shadows.'

'Money, money! Why does everything always come back to that? There's more important things in life—even you seem to think so! Why can't you put them before making money?'

'My dear, if we don't earn our keep we'll go bust. Then we'd have to sell the estate. Who knows what sort of people would buy it? Maybe the types who would do just the sort of thing we're trying so hard not to: "improve" the land as they put it, plant the moors with conifers, drain all the ponds, chop down trees. End result? A really great massacre as thousands of birds and animals lose their entire natural habitats, their age-old homes. How can you compare our need to trap a few surplus weasels and rats and foxes with *that*?'

'You're just cleverer at arguing than we are,' said Caroline stubbornly.

Lady Harryman leaned forward. 'Right. Well! But you can't be exactly stupid yourselves, having organized your . . . er, criminal activities so meticulously. OK, I admit I spend half my life on committees and so on trying to talk people into agreeing with me, but there's no reason why *you* can't learn to think things through properly and argue for them just as well. I'm—what—four times as old as you, but you're young, you lucky things, you've got plenty of time to find out, to practise, to learn!'

She held their astonished stares steadily with her own.

'Oh, for goodness' sake,' she said impatiently, 'haven't you got the intelligence to see that we're really on the same side? We both want to save animals, don't we? The only thing we can't agree on is how best to do it. You're obsessed with the little details, the odd individuals, because they're easy to see, you can identify with them personally, and they make you so angry—so you go round destroying things. But *I* say, the details don't matter, it's the overall pattern that's important. What matters above all to me, is not to destroy but to *save* things, the big things . . . I mean, to look after the whole shape of the countryside while there's still some of it left.

'Look, here's the natural scheme of things: a world where big strong creatures eat little weak ones, but all in the right balance for each to survive. Well, Hugh and I and our shooting friends and Bob Metcalfe whom you love to hate—we're no more than the other big, strong, hungry animals, so long as we keep things in the right balance, which I can assure you we try our utmost to do.'

Frances Harryman sat with her shrewd eyes fixed on them. At last she broke the tense silence with a soft whistle. From under the desk, the three dogs stirred themselves, stretched, ambled lazily towards her. She fondled them absently.

'Now—do you understand that your way of loving animals isn't the only one that's valid?'

Clearly she was waiting for an answer. Sarah glanced at her sister, but Caz was staring fixedly at the great spreading patches of damp their sodden clothes had made on the sofa. Resolutely, Sarah cleared her throat: at last her voice came.

'I . . . I think we understand . . . *I* do, anyway. And I'm ever so sorry for . . . the harm we've done.

Honestly.' She hesitated. 'Please are you going to have us arrested now?'

'Well,' said Lady Harryman, 'you're no better than common criminals. The police have been out hunting you. Yes, indeed.' She rubbed her chin thoughtfully. 'But it seems to me that having you arrested would be an utter waste of time and public money.'

Relief flooded through Sarah so fast that she wanted to faint.

'Why?' demanded Caroline defiantly.

'Because it would probably mess up your lives so much that it would stop you ever doing what you jolly well ought to do.'

'What do you mean?'

'I mean, you ought to learn how to talk sense!' said Lady Harryman crisply. 'Instead of all this half-garbled, fanatical nonsense. Make the effort to get your facts right. Then get off your backsides and work out how to change the world in a way that's really going to do some good—not acting like a couple of childish, dim-witted yobbos, smashing up private property. For goodness' sake, use your brains and initiative, use your passion constructively! You'll be grown up in a few years—then you can get out there and be campaigning properly for wildlife. But no one's going to listen to you if you don't know what you're talking about, or if you behave like a couple of good-for-nothing petty vandals!'

She stood up suddenly and threw open the door.

'Now get the hell out of here! Go on, we've said all there is to say.'

'You're going to let us go—free?' whispered Sarah incredulously.

'If Bob or I or Hugh or—woe betide—the police

catch you at your activities again, it'll be quite a different matter. But if it stops here and now, I couldn't even care less who you are.'

She strode out into the passage. White-faced, in a daze, Sarah and Caroline stood up and followed her out.

'I suppose you expect us to be grateful . . .' began Caroline.

'I don't expect you to be anything,' said Frances Harryman. 'All I ask is this: go away and *think* about it!'

And with that she shoved them firmly down the passage, out through the door—and slammed it shut behind them.